TRIPTYCH

Knock on the Heart:
love, love, love
4 / 24 / 2010

ALSO BY JEROME ROTHENBERG

POETRY

White Sun Black Sun (1960)
Between: Poems 1960–1963 (1967)
Poems 1964–1967 (1968)
Poems for the Game of Silence (1971)
Poland/1931 (1974)
A Seneca Journal (1978)
Vienna Blood (1980)
That Dada Strain (1983)
New Selected Poems 1970–1985 (1986)
Khurbn & Other Poems (1989)
The Lorca Variations (1993)
Gematria (1993)
Seedings & Other Poems (1996)
A Paradise of Poets (1999)
A Book of Witness (2003)

TRANSLATIONS

New Young German Poets (1959)
Hochhuth's "The Deputy," playing version
 (1965)
*Enzensberger's "Poems for People Who
 Don't Read Poems,"* with Michael
 Hamburger (1968)
*The Book of Hours & Constellations, or
 Gomringer by Rothenberg* (1968)
*The 17 Horse Songs of Frank Mitchell
 X-XIII* (1973)
15 Flower World Variations (1984)
*Schwitters' "Poems Performance Pieces
 Proses Plays Poetics (PPPPPP),"*
 with Pierre Joris (1993)
Lorca's "Suites" (2001)
Nezval's "Antilyrik & Other Poems,"
 with Milos Sovak (2001)
*Picasso's "The Burial of Count Orgaz &
 Other Poems,"* with Pierre Joris (2003)
*Writing Through: Translations &
 Variations* (2004)

ANTHOLOGIES

Technicians of the Sacred (1968, 1985)
Shaking the Pumpkin (1972, 1986)
America a Prophecy, with George Quasha
 (1973)
Revolution of the Word (1974)
A Big Jewish Book, with Harris Lenowitz
 and Charles Doria (1977)
Symposium of the Whole,
 with Diane Rothenberg (1983)
Exiled in the Word, with Harris Lenowitz
 (1989)
Poems for the Millennium (2 vols.),
 with Pierre Joris (1995 and 1998)
A Book of the Book, with Steven Clay
 (2000)

RECORDINGS

From a Shaman's Notebook (1968)
Origins & Meanings (1968)
Horse Songs & Other Soundings (1975)
6 Horse Songs for 4 Voices (1978)
Signature, with Charles Morrow (2002)

PROSE

Pre-Faces & Other Writings (1981)
The Riverside Interviews (1984)

JEROME ROTHENBERG

TRIPTYCH

POLAND/1931

◆

KHURBN

◆

THE BURNING BABE

**WITH A PREFACE
BY CHARLES BERNSTEIN**

A NEW DIRECTIONS BOOK

Book Design by Sylvia Frezzolini Severance
Manufactured in the United States of America
New Directions Books are printed on acid-free paper
First published as a New Directions Paperbook Original (NDP1077) in 2007
Published simultaneously in Canada by Penguin Books Canada Limited

Library of Congress Cataloging-in-Publication Data

Rothenberg, Jerome, 1931-
    Triptych / Jerome Rothenberg ; preface by Charles Bernstein.
        p. cm.
    Includes index.
    ISBN 978-0-8112-1692-0 (alk. paper)
    I. Rothenberg, Jerome, 1931- Poland/1931. II. Rothenberg, Jerome, 1931-Khurbn. III. Rothenberg, Jerome, 1931- Burning babe. IV. Title.
    PS3568.O86T79 2007
    811'.54—dc22
                                    2007004870

New Directions Books are published for James Laughlin
by New Directions Publishing Corporation,
80 Eighth Avenue, New York, NY 10011

CONTENTS

PREFACE

Before Auschwitz, the extermination camp was
unimaginable. Today, it can be imagined.
Because Auschwitz really happened, *it has permeated*
our imagination, become a permanent part of us.
                              —Imre Kertész

Jerome Rothenberg was born in America in 1931. That year, 1931, marks also the beginning of the poet's parallel, imaginative, investment in the Central European world of his parents, a world that had ceased to exist by the time Rothenberg had moved from babe to boy. *Triptych* is haunted by this double consciousness. It is as if written from the other side of this imaginative divide, so that the dead might come back and speak to us:

> saddlesore I came
> a jew among
> the indians
> vot em I doink in dis strange place
> mit deez pipple mit strange eyes
> could be it's trouble
> could be   could be

The poems in *Triptych* envision a place neither there nor here: they build a liminal dwelling of betweenness, populated by ghosts and goblins, where objects are disguised as words and words are used as objects of resistance. All of this is presided over by historical personages brandishing indelible facts and syncretic figures making the only sense we may know this side of Heaven.

The Jewish world of Poland, evoked in the first poems of this collection, survives in three magical places: the historical record; the memories and testimonies of survivors from the time; and works of the imagination, such as *Poland/1931*. *Triptych* is both a testimony to, and proof of, the necessity of imaginative acts over, and indeed against, fixed memorials. Its three-part structure works as a counter to the binary thinking of good/bad, us/them, here/there, light/dark, theism/disbelief. In these poems, Rothenberg swerves away from binary thinking toward the dialogic, toward, that is, a third term that is always on the horizon but never grasped. In this way, Rothenberg forces lyric poetry to splinter into songs, like sparks escaping from fire. With the full force of lyric enunciation, *Triptych* articulates the otherness of the known and the familiarity of that which is foreign.

Rothenberg's poetry actively resists closure, unity of design, and singleness of method. The commitment is to viscerally grapple with that which is difficult to confront and impossible to contain in any single image or icon. In the trilogy, Rothenberg employs an exemplary range of styles: there is no one voice, no one kind of representation. Indeed, *Triptych* is full of radical changes of perspective, angle, tone, and format that never entirely add up so as to better remain restlessly on the move, troubled as much as troubling. For this is a poetics of discrepancy rather than mimesis.

Rothenberg notes in his preface to *Khurbn*, the second poem of the trilogy, that he visited Poland for the first time in 1987 and that he could only find there, then, ghost traces of the Poland that he had so memorably brought to life in *Poland/1931*. This absence, the vanishing of the Jewish world and the negation of any way to make sense of the agency that caused it, is at the heart of *Khurbn*.

Khurbn is one of the few American poems to figure the systematic extermination of the European Jews. Yet, so much depends upon the terms of this figuring. In *Khurbn*, Rothenberg turns Adorno not so much on his head as on his side. Negative dialectics (the negation of any expressive representation) is the poet's starting point, since there is never a question of representing the totality of the desecration. But Rothenberg moves from the groundlessness of negative dialectics toward a series of concrete expressions, notations, responses, and images, that are serially constelled in a way that never fails to open onto a void or negation or absence:

> They covered the mirrors with towels, drew the blinds,
> knocked over the chairs, broke the dishes, & stopped
> the clock. Then he put on a pair of felt slippers, to
> accompany the coffin.

The method is already anticipated in "The Annunciation," Rothenberg's 1968 working of a Tibetan source in *Poems for the Game of Silence*:

> a man without lips who is speaking who
> sees without eyes a man without ears
> who listens who runs without legs

Khurbn was written in the late 1980s, when Rothenberg was in his late fifties. In his preface for this volume, Rothenberg writes that in *Poland/1931* he had come up to the edge of the catastrophe but had not gone over it. This conscious, and no doubt unconscious, refusal or evasion or "repression of war experience" (to use the title of Siegfried Sassoon's haunting poem) is an acknowledgment that the modes of representation available or even inventible were inadequate or themselves evasive or repressive of the trauma.

The problem is inherent even in the name. The extermination of the European Jews was not a sacrifice, which is why *Shoah*, a Hebrew word meaning "catastrophe," is often used in preference to *holocaust*. Rothenberg, however, uses a Yiddish word, *khurbn*, meaning "destruction," which retains, for him, the power of the vernacular.

Triptych ends with *The Burning Babe*, a series written, very consciously, in the first years of a new millennium and some of which was first published in an illuminated book with a Pandora's box of vivid images by Susan Bee.

Who is "the burning babe"?

No doubt it is the poet's doppelganger, the Jewish baby born in Poland in 1931.

The baby as ash, negation, empty, hollow (and so as *alter* Christ).

Ghost, avatar.

Who can speak for this infant?

It is not as if Rothenberg asked for the assignment. He was chosen.

These poems are everywhere in touch with what Stevens calls "the pressure of reality." And wherever this pressure is felt, you will find a hole.

Where there is no possibility of a whole, there dwells the holy.

MORNING
"But that which weeps is the mind."

The Burning Babe becomes cinders in the holocaust of our imagination. We have been forced to imagine the unimaginable and face that which we cannot give a face (Demon, Golem, the Dark). The burden for poetry after Auschwitz may be as much what we have to unimagine—negate—as what we must reimagine, in other words, reconfigure and reconceive. This is the ethical foundation of Jerome Rothenberg's stunning series, *Triptych*.

Charles Bernstein
New York, September 11, 2006

TRIPTYCH

POLAND/1931

. . . And I said, "O defiled flock, take a harp, & chant
to the ancient relics, lest understanding perish."
—E. DAHLBERG

POLAND/1931

POLAND/1931   "The Wedding"

my mind is stuffed with tablecloths
& with rings but my mind
is dreaming of poland stuffed with poland
brought in the imagination
to a black wedding
a naked bridegroom hovering above
his naked bride   mad poland
how terrible thy jews at weddings
thy synagogues with camphor smells & almonds
thy thermos bottles thy electric fogs
thy braided armpits
thy underwear alive with roots o poland
poland poland poland poland poland
how thy bells wrapped in their flowers toll
how they do offer up their tongues to kiss the moon
old moon old mother stuck in thy sky thyself
an old bell with no tongue a lost udder
o poland thy beer is ever made of rotting bread
thy silks are linens merely thy tradesmen
dance at weddings where fanatic grooms
still dream of bridesmaids still are screaming
past their red moustaches poland
we have lain awake in thy soft arms forever
thy feathers have been balm to us
thy pillows capture us like sickly wombs & guard us
let us sail through thy fierce weddings poland

let us tread thy markets where thy sausages grow ripe & full
let us bite thy peppercorns let thy oxen's dung be sugar to
      thy dying jews
o poland o sweet resourceful restless poland
o poland of the saints unbuttoned poland repeating endlessly
      the triple names of mary
poland poland poland poland poland
have we not tired of thee poland no for thy cheeses
shall never tire us nor the honey of thy goats
thy grooms shall work ferociously upon their looming brides
shall bring forth executioners
shall stand like kings inside thy doorways
shall throw their arms around thy lintels poland
& begin to crow

THE KING OF THE JEWS

Is a stranger. Is
Sharp. Cries
For fish. Is wanting
A wristwatch.

A Poultice. One
Bathes. One intrudes
On the Nightwatch.
One steals.

Catch him. He slips
From your nets. Anoint

Him. The father of weights.
Brother of Edom.

One is a practical man.
One protects. One
Gathers. The table is set.
Find platters.

Find ostriches. Hair
Is refinement.
For thieves. For widows.
A stitch is copper.

One cuts. Makes fingers
That button. He
Suits us. Soon
He is fed.

He is heavy. One
Sings for him. Bathes
In his room.
One counts sheets for him.

Is a steward. Is
Dull. Begs
For soup. Is wanting
A hatband.

One steals. One adds numbers.
He testifies. What
Is a number past one.
A number.

THE KEY OF SOLOMON

tallow tongues of oxen cock messias sorrel pox a glass
a root a dish an open dish a cockatrice a ring a key:

From the skin of a hare
the blood of a black hen
or a newly killed sheep
& occasionally the meat of animals & birds
the food is steamed with pleasant odors.
Stand at the eastern corner.
Bless this carpet.
Burn a dove's feather.
Point to westward.
Afflict the knees
& tyrannize over cats.
This is the ring of travel.
This is the yellow cloth
that causes love between two people.
From this will be made an ink.
From this a square.
A turtle.
Take a chain, a hook & the figure of a bird.
Make a talisman of leather.
& a white vessel.
This is the ring of incest
"the needle of the art."
Its signs are seven.

> *Saturn, black.*
> *Jupiter, azure blue.*
> *Mars, red.*
> *Sun, gold or yellow.*

Venus, green.
Mercury, mixed.
Moon, silver or white gray.

& it is said in The Book of Beasts
that the lizard fleeth the privvy members of a man
therefore when they see it
they bind ropes from the male to the female
& bow down to the male.

SATAN IN GORAY

An Homage to Isaac Bashevis Singer

1
Sect.
Avert sect.
Avert to wash bellies.
Sect.
Avert sect.

2
Worship.
Womanly
Towns & Towns.
Tones.
Witness.
Witness & Witness.
Woman redeemed.

Woman redeemed woman redeemed.

3
Crutches.
Crutches cockcrow.
Crutches cockcrow Jews.
Crutches impure.
Crutches impure cockcrow.
Crutches Jews.

4
Drinking.
Drinking in devil.
Prayers.
Prayerful.

5
Messiah.
First a holiday malice.
Abyss.
Ark bares Levi.

6
Sabbath.
Sabbatai Zevi.
Sodom Sodom.
Sodom Sodom.

7
Marriage bed marriage bed.
Brittle.
Marriage breasts.

Marriage breasts bristle.
Match me.
Onan.
Again.
Pederasty.
In Three.

8

Fat yes fat yes fat yes idol. Fat yes fat yes fat yes idol.

9

Something is Presence.

10

Holy Muhammed.

11

Pass over.
Pass over.
Pass.
Pass.
Pass.
Pass.
Pass pass.   (G. Stein)

Pass water.

12
Lilith a red head.
Jest nudgingly.
S & Z & S & Z.   S & Z & S & Z.   S & Z & S & Z.   Selah.

SOAP (I)

The lonely. Sliding
between my hands
A sorrowful island
he dreams of small birds in fragments above his head
& smeared windows
misted eyeglasses
something white floating in a tumbler
lips drinking
remembering a silence white as soap
like rubbing out a name
"the man who writes his name
                         on the beloved's belly"
knows it
what does the man know
hiding from a name?

Answer: "the place where it was hidden"

wax. Sweet
scent
an open skylight
soap

a hand against the tap, palm flat
delight of using soap
he opens papers
sometimes he throws away the ribbon
& picks his nose
Soap in all his orifices
he says, Someone
is clean
Even the doorknob smells of soap

SOAP (II)

Will the man who gets clean love his neighbor?
Yes the facts are apparent yes the facts
live on in the mind if the mind lives on
"I have no right to another man's business
& it makes me sick"
When Meyer fell asleep in his chair, his wife shouted DON'T
    TOUCH MEYER!
The sugar at the bottom of his cup was brown & hard
Twice a month he had the hairs clipped from his nose
& thanked his barber
(he had sold him shaving soap the day before)
Selling soap to the pious
calling it *zeyf*
saying: *ah shtick zeyf*
or saying: *ah shtickeleh zeyf* (dim.)
theirs was a business between friends
& meant lying

But the tips of his fingers smellt good to him
women admired it
the books on his shelf were in a language he couldn't
        understand
So he began to make little songs
& to stuff his pockets with little bars of soap
"Children, eat omelets
"Children, when the chamberpots are empty the great bear comes
        at night
"Children, there are other values in this life"
Yes said the voices in his dream yes
sang the voices to the man who sold soap
& was ticklish
But where will the road end, do the voices
tell you where the road will end
Do they lead you to a new town where the people aren't clean?
"I have no right to another man's business
& it makes me sick"
There were always towns like that

THE CONNOISSEUR OF JEWS

if there were locomotives to ride home on
& no jews
there would still be jews & locomotives
just as there are jews & oranges
& jews & jars
there would still be someone to write the jewish poem
others to write their mothers' names in light—

just as others, born angry
have the moon's face burnt onto their arms
& don't complain
my love, my lady, be a connoisseur of jews
the fur across your lap
was shedding
on the sheet were hairs
the first jew to come to you is mad
the train pulls into lodz
he calls you
by your polish name
then he tells the other passengers a story
there are jews & there are alphabets
he tells them
but there are also jewish alphabets
just as there are jewish locomotives
& jewish hair
& just as there are some with jewish fingers
such men are jews
just as other men are not jews
not mad
don't call you by your polish name
or ride the train to lodz
if there are men who ride the train to lodz
there are still jews
just as there are still oranges
& jars
there is still someone to write the jewish poem
others to write their mothers' names in light

THE MOTHERS

1
scandal, too hard to bear
but kept in her mind
from girlhood   it returned
& hung around the bed
somebody's mouth was always going
words in the old tongue
language of the simple people of our town
there ought to be a book
if someone would ever learn to write with light
& burn it in my heart
that was the way we learnt our history
but forgot it
learnt to unscramble simple sentences
& as a girl husht it up

2
mothers first
& dancers in love with misfortune
together we sat
together we told the bushes the names of our loves
a spy?
a squadron of guards from the palace?
a dirigible back of the lake?
all is secret, sing the mothers
all is innocent
& draws a white circle
behind their eyes
the circle starts to swell   moistens
& leaves a trail of fat
how beautiful, she says

3
she has their desire to be always in love
always respectable
as if prosperity were the name of a town
or of a house in the town
& had no windows
"doomed to old age, they withered"
went the song   the secret was out
there will be no sun from this day forward
no more numbers to add up
or coins embedded in the risen dough
all is done, sing the mothers
all is forgiven
& has no book of its own written in light
& no town

POLAND / 1931   "The Fish"

the dead fish has no eyes
says my son, poland
has no eyes
& so we live without associations
in the past we live
nourishing incredible polands
lazy & alive remembering
our mothers' pictures in the grass
this is the jewish poem
not being jewish much less
being polish
much less being human

we are miles away
& we move toward something unmistakably
alive & fat
a tender treasure an illusion
how clean we are
we sing   the fathers
having once been insistent
now turn deaf
they open stores in kansas
dream of links
to china secret cargoes
with a mad impulse to buy & sell
some mark a pause between occasions
like a holiday a wedding
more like a game of chess
wherein the figure
holding up the queen
leans over   dies
but leaves a hole for sleep

THE GRANDMOTHERS

1
a man & a woman smiling   coming
to fulfillment in a picture
at the end of a long table with white
tablecloth   impossibly broad spoons   bread
the length of a ladder
brown & shining would delight

the grandmothers their little parched
hands holding handkerchiefs
noses fight back tears at memory of
veiled hats hidden
in the closet getting old escaping
the fond picture she grows down
to death but won't admit it
for the bride & groom

2

the oldest woman in the world kicks off
her shoes   dances on the table
she chews fat & garlic wipes bread
around the rim of plate & croaks
for water at midnight
the sleep of the grandmothers is broken
by laughter small voices from inside
the bathhouse call to her   animals invade
her bed comfortable fur
wraps around her & makes her snore
but knowing no woman will ever be clean
she blows her nose to clear it
one hand between her thighs   rinses the tight
membrane   still combs the knots out of her hair

3

past caring a grandmother
bathing checks mucus in her eyes dough
on her hands shit between
asshole & water dirt under her fingernails
her false teeth backed with gold

wax in ears snot in nose lice at pubis
still seeking to be pure the residue
of past bleedings buried with her sons
but fresh in mind she yawns from
drowsiness sometimes or belches after meals
in pain her legs feel heavy a blood spot
whirls before her   inserts a soft
white woolen cloth the cock's remembered
length inside her that returns in whiteness

4
the men by custom wait outside
her door even the young boys grandchildren
for whom the alphabet flowers in hebrew
"have respect for the body of a grandmother
"have respect for the vessel of blood
"emptied   bearer of offspring from her damp nostrils"
in the small rooms where the grandmothers
sleep they are still women
still withdrawn   glowing   in the mystery
that forbids us to drink from her cup
keeps her mattress in the center of the room
forever keeps her blood away from us
as softly the curtain flutters on her wedding night
something between a woman & a man

"The Beards"

the idea of geometry is like the idea
of beards an idea of how the light
striking his eyeglasses makes the beards
that hang from their faces
brush the sky   a neglected dream of beards
mad Shimeon saw in their glory
sitting in a house of beards holding
the long hairs in his fist
winding & unwinding hanks of beard
oh beards I was your good shepherd once I was
the guardian of all your ringlets
king of beards & eyebrows king of armpits
beards were everywhere we turned
our hands grew beards palms bore the mouths of bearded women
mothers whose emblems were a goat & a baboon
who sang about beards & kingdoms old songs of home
impossible avenues forbidden towns where beards grow
hair grew in unmixed colors there was wisdom
in kisses charity spoke first from beards
but was rebuffed by strangers polacks appeared in gangs
ran us through the dawn the sun striking against Shimeon's
uplifted eyes who hoarse in praise of beards
made it to the railroad yards but perished
"oh beards I love you beards
"beards which are concealed & beards which show
"beards which begin at earline & go down
"to mouth descending & ascending covering
"the cheeks with fragrance white with ornament
"& balanced to the breastline
"beards of thirteen fountains   sources   dispositions

"first the ears
"second the corners of the mouth
"third between the nostrils
"fourth beneath the mouth from one corner to the other
"fifth also beneath the mouth   a tuft
"sixth ascending from below then rises to the corners fragrant at the
     upper edges
"seventh where it ends two apples grow
"eighth a tress encircling it
"ninth mingled with the eighth but braided
"tenth the tongue uncovered the hair surrounding it is lovely
"eleventh above the throat
"twelfth the fringes at its base are knotted
"thirteenth hair hanging down both sides a covering for the chest
besides the hair down from his shoulders pure
hippie god of light pure beard & hair
his lineage is in his face a hint of kingship
knowing no god without a beard
he curls the lowest hairs thinks about tomorrow
runs tongue around lips or presses
cool pillow to burning cheeks
a phallic beard is his but on a woman's
          face
                    someone calls him
mother of the gentiles others
          are bringing lentils to his room
                    still others are kissing his wet hairs
that none will be dishonored none more rich or beautiful
          than these   my strength is in my beard
                    he cries my life is in it

how many would die rather than have their beards cut?

THE FATHERS

1

some were in love & grew
beautifully in the half darkness of the home
for which they lit candles
& waited still confident of business
hot for betrayals & clarity
"the vision" was its name in the old books
the title stuck only the streets
were those of a small western town in august
& some who could hardly breathe there
grew more restless still   settled
in vipertown   filled the whole country
with clothes & their dream of zion
the woman   breasts hanging down to her palms
fixed breakfast   "perfectly content to be your friend

2

the merchant with the pink thick lips
& little hanging moustache
laying tiles for you or measuring your neck
to suit you or speaking to your wife
the fat he sold you sputtering in the pan
& later   cold & white   filling a milk container
smelling of injuries & flies   was rich
but took the stagecoach regularly
to tombstone or other western towns
short of cash or pissing on the wall
back of his store   started to masturbate
a gentleman his father told him

learns to sit on air   the manners of the gentiles
haunt him   Be a brother to your wife

3
some broke through a wall   others
fatter with a smell of fish
around their lips threatened & choked
eager lovely forgetful violent
they waited at the dock
some told them it was nearly daylight
others didn't know & others
spoke of the night as though they lived in it
in love with colors some were tolerant
of sleep but nervous at remembrance
some were kings others knew kings
& dreamed about the weather
when it rained our fathers left their cities
as we were always being told

MILK & HONEY

1
Milk freezes overnight
& the skin feels it
First as a question of color & number
For reasons other than health
Or because no one else would take a chance on it
Later, having entered a home

It is easier to talk
This is your uncle, speak to him
A little
He prefers to drink milk
Says it reminds him of his wounds
& shows them
We were always close friends
Never more than that
What does it matter if his heart is good
A warm spot in my heart for him

2
Honey is practical
A device sometimes for cooling
Called honey-that-cools
Or white honey
It makes a thin line around the mouth
The color of honey matters less
But its taste is a honey taste
Always
For the man who tells you, Jews
Eat honey
You must have a ready answer
Tell him
It makes a thin line around the mouth
& tastes sweet

THE BROTHERS

to live with potatoes   not to eat them
but to live with them
they each had identical desires
& would surprise the neighbors by bellowing
if someone was good he was also
first & practical
wore long coats but kept the buttons
in his pockets   would paste
dollar bills in the pages of his books
while saying
                    the music that he heard
was "really" music   how are brothers
different? everyone would ask
the world would never recognize his beauty
found him "without love but blameless"
never certain who was walking beside him
he let his daughters dream about his sons
& vanished   it was nearly Spring
but not in Poland
brothers everywhere ran through the snow
spitting, my father said
they let the ice form on their hands
but more a question of politics
than of possessions   each man made his way
badly
grew up to lose a wad of cash
brothers with faces that were always old
they tried to sleep at odd hours
one masturbated to the age of fifty
smiling   one was always telling time

a loser's life
the brother sank deeper into his own business
at night the table danced   the house
had nearly come alive
& was dangerous
there was nothing to talk about so he listened
stunned by the taste of food
a fire in his jaw   here was his father
selling gloves again
one morning he saw a rooster in the elevator
could he think of names for it?
Aladdin
Abba
Ahasuerus
every name he knew started with "a"
& pained him
now it pained him even more
he thought   the world
stopped being round or holding snow
women, slightly crazed
met him in the streets   daubed his hands
with goatshit
this was the key to paradise   the names
of paradise
were written in his heart
his brother told him
they were standing at a window crying
from their mouths
brothers have names to tell their shoes by
not their own   they were always old

A POEM FOR THE CHRISTIANS

the skull   the air   the fire
the holy name
but destitute of good works
in a land that was not sown for us
& on the sabbath day
two buicks of the previous year
without blemish
& two tenth parts of rubber
for a meal offering
mingled with gasoline
& chrome
this is the burnt offering of
every sabbath
for which rabbi yosi
left us
& rabbi abba came in his place
to praise the president
(selah)
our mouths are full of songs
(selah)
our hands hold offerings
the grieving bear   the moth
the leopard
the seven kinds of quantity & six kinds of motion
& on the sabbath day
black bodies &
bodies green with oil
& bodies gone for a burnt offering
two tenth parts for the buick
& one tenth part for the rambler

& one tenth part
for every lamb of the seven lambs
(selah)
& for their jewish god

POLAND / 1931   "The Bride"

o Shekinah o thou my defeated flower
trampled my Bessarabian daisy by the boots of strangers
cossacks have struck their cocks on thee
on thy thighs have slept generations of tartars
what bitter exiles have brought thee to this bed
to leathern blankets aflake in Polish air
contamination of lungs o my Slavic moongirl
my bride where hast thou gone then
& wherefore wherefore hast left thy milk bottles behind
thy tits will I squeeze upon for wisdom
of a milk that drops like letters
sacred alphabet soup we lap up o thou my Shekinah
do not be thus far from us in our Galician wildernesses
who scratch under our prayervests alive alive
in dream of Shekinah's entry to the tents of God
one Sabbath with not prunes to eat but grapes
would crush them on the tongue of Him
shoot colors down his beard light bursts of sex
of lightbulbs colors in the flesh of brides their marriages
to light ordained from Paradise o thou Shekinah
o daughter spread on table
with red & yellow drops thy cunt doth come undone

with drops of soul purple & black drops thy children
spring to life in thee
great is thy womb a wedding hall for saints
silken men shall dance in shall bring their beards to thee
under thy tongue shall eat in Paradise thy fat buns
& know no separation male & female
shall be one in thee
in thee the fingers of God shall come together
shall know themselves in thee o Hole o Holy Mother
o Shekinah who seeketh thy happy home around the bend
& wilt thou find it now will the memory be gone for thee
gone the forced nights in Polish brothels the whip of the delighted
    nobles
on thy ass brought low brought to thy knees in sucking homage
o cunt of God o Goddess o thou egg thou albumen
thou eye thou semen spurt thou lip thou whisper o rising into
    scream
thou my SHEKINAH nerve of Elohim o soul I will split thee now
    into different-colored souls
will spread thee on a white cloth under lock & key
in a cabinet inside thy father's house
then will I watch the children coming from your womb God's
    keyhole
soul of Shekinah o soul of golden eels
where have I lost thee in what victory gardens hast thou gone astray
thy feminine body shall I make a table from
in name of Aleph of the bride shall spread a white soul on our tables
with also thy red & yellow black & purple spotted white & soft
    souls
o hermaphrodite will we not bring thee balm
will wipe our essence clean upon thee
like God will cry to thee "dear child dear daughter & dear wife
"never saw a good looking woman in this world"

thou motherer o thou dear universal ass & thighs
dear light dear earth of Elohim the crown
thou hijacked innocence in flight
when will we land in what America
shall be our resting place from what cruel Polands
the angel of the exile sings above our heads & stoops
& stooping down the golden table holds you
stooping down the golden table
the song of forgotten angels in thy throat
o hymn of Shekinah on her last night from home

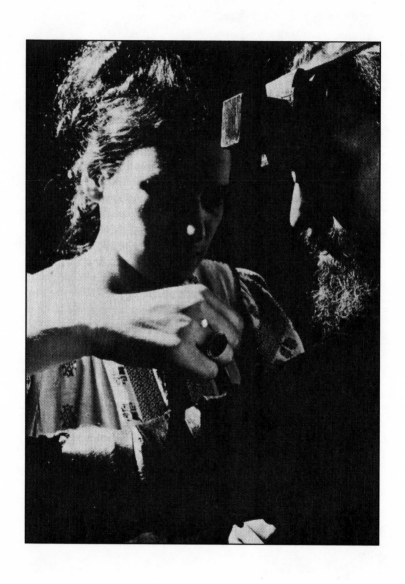

A BOOK OF TESTIMONY

THE BEADLE'S TESTIMONY

The boy who throws the ball
A jewel of a boy
His coat down to his feet
Earlocks flying

He will grow up to sell candles
Will eat a dog
& thrive on fat cigars
He will bless his mother too

Yes we are simple people
Yes we drive carts
& work with shit
Sometimes we study

Sometimes a fish in the hand
Sometimes charity
Eros is the Warsaw banker
Spain is far away

Kansas City is also far away
Where did our love go?
I have two hands & only one wallet
I want to speak to you about it

Cities & Jews
Walls & what is behind a wall
A temple sometimes
Sometimes a shining diesel locomotive

Sometimes charity
A boy's shadow on the wall
A jewel of a boy
He will grow up to sell candles

He will bless his mother too

THE STEWARD'S TESTIMONY

          master-of-the-household
    fat old jew
called *baal* the old king's
      name
   his fingers
blossomed in the earth dark flowers
       covered the bannisters
    women in white kerchiefs
running to cut them loose
       he was suffering from exhaustion
    having kicked hell out of her sides
the night before
       his teeth had cracked against the firm white
    buttocks
crying "power" "power"
       had tried to spread the cheeks apart

make the double entry
in god's name
                or by names
        hidden & lost
a man might die to know the secret of
                he spit against the hole
        quivered
was waiting for her hand
                to find him
        "how i do love thee, becky
"sweet rebekkah
                "rifkeh
        "descended from a line of lublin rabbis
"rose of the dispersion
                "yuh-buh-buh-buh-bum"
        the sight of his own penis
made him sick
                a swollen toad
        it squatted on his belly it was
toothless
                it puffed
        & trembled
her hand closed around it like a goose's neck
                licked its red mouth with her cowtongue
        mumbled "bridegroom"
"pig's balls"
                "little lamp of love"
        hossana!
the first busload of campers was leaving for the woods
                around him eyes
        watched from the house's open sides
schoolboys broke in
                flattened their palms against his
        ass & pressed him down

the bride
                    nibbled their earlocks
          pulled the kerchiefs from their necks
beat her own head against the wall the gilded paper
                    fell off in strips
          the glass case
splintered
                    sending a smell of spices
          through the room the glimmer
of his riches
                    silver candlesticks
          cups
candelabra
                    beakers
          vases
crystal
                    colored glass
          an umbrella with a silver handle
happiness
                    had come to the home of
          the timber merchant
humming the eighteen benedictions
                    he entered
          numerals in ledgers fingered
his spent cock maddened
                    by his dream of a northern forest
          lumberyards
not synagogues
                    were where he worshipped
          trains run by german
engineers led to his ark
                    "the wilderness"
          the buzz of saws
to witness a new kabbala

          whirred in his ears the young bride
     wrapped a kerchief
over his shrunken balls
        before he stopped her
     stuffed her hole with meat
naked
        they raced down hallways plundered
     her father's
holy relics
        pieces of amber on which the long dead
     maggid of kozhenitz
had said prayers
        fragments of black sugar which had touched
     the lips of the saintly
grandfather of shpoleh
        dried herbs
     parchment
strings of wolves' teeth
        black devil-fingers
     girdles of remnant strips
blesséd oil from the holy city of safad in the holy land
        they smeared on their bodies
     or drank
his grey beard fell on his chest
        a prayershawl across
     his belly
worms sang psalms from his navel the folds
        of loose fat
     hung like dough
his penis drew back
        & vanished
     redemption was his name for it
in our larders
        (hidden)

                    i would watch them tearing the raw
flesh they caught a calf
                    & butchered it
          smearing themselves with blood & fat
(he would drink the residue
                    called "life)
          stuck chickenfeathers to their thighs &
screamed like crows
                    not like an old man
          & his bride
the timber merchant drew heat from
                    the law
          at night he saw a mooncalf heard
distant trains
                    push toward silesia
          bought sausage from the gentiles
would drop it in the sabbath pots
                    or break into the synagogue & steal
          the prepuces of newborn infants
paradise
                    was on the road to lomza
          a tavern where the gentiles
danced for him
                    young girls opened their blouses & stood
          naked would hold their breasts up
to his lips
                    nipples the shape of acorns
          apple-colored
mushrooms between their legs
                    "how i adore defilement"
          he would cry & daub
his phylacteries with goatshit
                    later they washed his beard
          with kvass the odors

slid into his nose
                    & made him choke
        the way home
frightened him he heard voices
                    speaking turkish
        coins rolled helplessly from his pockets
& crossed the road
                    he found the back door
        open in the pantry
skirts above her hips
                    the housemaid
        sat eyes blinded
the young bride's head moved slowly
                    in her lap a dead song
        dribbled from the timber merchant's
gums he blessed the walls but couldn't
                    find his stick
        his skullcap
fell into the soup
                    the broom had grown a mouth
        teeth he didn't know
were biting him
                    sobbing
        he learned to fly would later
become an owl
                    companion for the grandmothers in the woods
        "redeemed" "redeemed"
the timber merchant cried
                    bandits & martyrs were dancing
        with the moon they hailed him
as their king
                    but homesick
        in his wilderness
transfigured or crushed

          flowering or awash
      his fingers tore at his belly mangled
the folds of flesh
         the dark wounds
     blossomed he visited
the wooded shrines around the town
          & raged there
     would make up names
to suit himself
          "master-of-the-household"
   "cat"
"fat face"
      "blossomer"
   "the stump"
"the swallower of millions"

THE RABBI'S TESTIMONY

They are deceived under their hats
Because they wear them
Old men with green faces
& young men with faces growing testy

All will come at me & whisper
Rabbi, rabbi sit with us
Make our associations pleasant
For a glass of unmixed honey

How can I answer for a town of ghosts?
My lips are blue from it
Also my balls are blue
From someone's endless testimony

The rabbi will walk up & down among your women
& will pretend a birth in old age
Some days he will gamble
Others he will learn to hump among the Poles

Oh hump hump lump bump thump
The rabbi breaks his balls to save you
& is often cursed
Nightly the golden vessel bursts in two

The substance splatters
At the door called sleep he waits for you
He knows the goddess of the gentiles
But names her Sabbath

Heavy, cold, delicious, bewildered
Flowering, wounded in his nature
Not wounded really but not intact
He is not wounded or intact

But thinking: Rabbi, rabbi
Sometimes he spends his winters in Miami
These are the net benefits of love
Our fathers called disaster

THE SLAUGHTERER'S TESTIMONY

         impeccable zeal
    of a slaughterer
his delight in the passage of generations
        or in a bull's
    pizzle
purity of his knives
        of all shapes & sizes
    & other commandments
with one eye closed
        one eye open the great slaughterer
    leans across the white
washed table powerful
        in kashrut balancing
    a drop of blood on thumbnail his kaftan
lifted high
        spits on the black whetstone
    the green stone to polish with
white belgian stones his bookseller
        brings him
    he dreams of small executions
animals that call him from sleep
        pink flesh drawn tight under
    his palm
a length of gums a black lip
        hanging loose
    skin swinging free in two directions
his fingers
        probe the mesentery
    warts
on a goat's intestines
        could destroy a world

                    blood in milk
in eggs the blood
                         from his own gums
             weaken a slaughterer cause the sinew
of the hip to shrink from him
                         creeping things
              to settle into the legs
of his table
                         as into flesh
             spoiling his buckwheat
at nightfall the mothers
                         come to him
             widows bring loaves
for the sabbath
                         the examiner beside them
             to poke & test to ask questions
still uncertain
                         brides leave the bathhouse
             unwashed & smelling of
his racks their blood
                         sticks to his eyelids
             blinds him
the table & the walls turn red
                         his heart explodes against
             his belt
buckle
                         forcing the sugar to his throat
             red lumps
the unclean mice were carrying to their holes
                         the unclean camels
             offered him their livers
mouthed his woolen fringes with red froth
                         red slime of slugs
             red weasel tongues

red pelicans
              red eyes of cormorants
      red bats
the slaughterer falls backwards where a second
           slaughterer
      waits in the basement of
a synagogue he mustn't enter
           but prays there
      in the name of pig
with knives around his neck but
           blunted caked with fat
      smelling of sweat
the intruder pisses blindly puts
           his own penis on
      the chopping block
his balls are hairy like a lamb's
           blue veins tightening with
      premonitions drops of blood
red jewels
           circle the cock's rim
      little isaac
dances for his father the covenant
           blossoms
      reaches as far as poland
where crowned &
           beautiful the last
      empress of the gentiles
hands him his knives
           shining them up with
      albumen his finger
up her hole he blows
           two trumpets
      butchers
the maimed calf scraping

                    scabs from its eyes
                becomes a meat god
        bellows in the name of
                        animal & other
                untasted powers of the earth
        processions from the woods
                        that threaten him
                crying
        for murder of lost children in the other's
                        dream a slaughterer escapes
                a slaughterer
        splits his own skull open removing
                        the brain
                pulling tubes from his lungs
        fat & veins
                        from spleen then spills
                milk from his stomach
        hanging himself from a hook
                        a martyr to kashrut
                he will sit at the foot of the law
        in paradise
                        slitting the monsters' throats
                will geld behemoth
        throw his balls across the thousand
                        mountains will tie
                leviathan's tongue down
        with a rope
                        thrust a reed
                through his nostrils
        a thorn between his jaws
                        will snare the reem
                that wild ox whose shit
        made jordan overflow
                        while fearful

beneath his brows the lowest
angel helps him feed
                    blood to the zealous
        merchants & small artisans
ranged like the letters on god's forehead
                    mumbling THE NAME THE NAME
        in hebrew
& other holy tongues some stammering
                    in russian
        but whose words are turned to
gold
                    gleaming like drops of
        fat from fingers
of a slaughterer they wipe like
                    cherubims' on beards
        eternal napkins
prayers glowing from the warming pans
                    where even the pious drink the blood
        of angels keeping
a universe alive

THE STUDENT'S TESTIMONY

                    he was the last demon of ostrow
        come back to visit & play
on my mind blowing delicious
                    bubbles of red soap into
        the corners of the room
a furry singing little
                    demon with bulging eyes big

bulging balls & all
animal twisted into shapes
                    like rubber
"I love my demon" I would sing
& we would share the backroom of
                    the synagogue guzzling
          the gentiles' beer &
snapping paperclips
                    against the rabbi's silks reliving
          the poland of old friendships pork & fish
boiling & stinking in a single
                    pot we would dip our hands
          into & make our bellies
shine
                    what grease
          what aromas from the bookshelves
what smells of jews ripe for the sabbath
                    "fur" I would cry to him or "snot" & he
          would wrap me in his sleeves & let
their velvet warm me
                    nightly the books were opening
          in my dreams the letters
black as coal danced off
                    the page & fell on me I saw them
          cross my hips & write the double
yod upon my cock
                    "never had polish child felt
          greater warmth beside her
mother than I felt there"
                    later the telephone came voices
          reached us from "the kingdoms"
messages of love
                    vibrated there were calls
          from warsaw krakow moscow kiev odessa

paris berlin new york london
        buenos aires hong kong yokahama bombay
    melbourne juneau tombstone perth
detroit johannesburg topeka east st louis
        homesick we dreamed "freedom" meaning
    that our hands could touch our feet reach
even the dirt between
      the toes
    & breathe its essence
(of a hundred slaughterhouses
      the sweet fat of the sabbath
    in our teeth we waited until the women
came to us bearing the bloody eyes
      of cows & lambs
    they piled up on the table crying
"hossana to the gentiles")
      buckwheat for dinner
    in the lonely diner
eating globs of fat congealed
      we played games near wealthy
    homes pretending that we were children
"the luck of the jews"
      "constantinople nights"
    "making the devil's mark on parchment"
also "the hair & beard of macroanthropos"
      through which he led me his
    furry body hidden under
three suits of clothes towards other
      pleasures secret holes
    he lived in
bathhouse partitions white with mold
      & through a broken board the eye
    watched the old women strove to behold
the slit the fiery entranceway

dissolve
the waters washing out the light the breath
that moves upon the waters
until the bulb above us splintered
"god is one"
we sang my demon clung to me
made of my tongue
his song
a master at pinochle sometimes
the deck flew in his hands
beautiful men wept like children
some shelled almonds for him
or filled his hat with vodka
the fat students loved him the dark ones
waited for news on the radio
"calm in the face of disaster"
pilgrims visited the tsaddik's court he sat
for seven days
dipped figs in wine
then lifted his milkwhite hands each
finger held a garnet
each eye a golden tear
electricity ran from his beard he wore
a neon caftan
thrice did my demon limp into his presence
they were face-to-face neither
moving neither still in love
or heartsick
theirs was a meeting of the upper
& the lower worlds
the "model of the universe" was always
at their call an empty building windows
broken or taped-up with X's
in contrast to the tsaddik's its

easy warmth stoves in perfect order
so even a stranger had a place to sit
                    forgetful of each other
         they let the time pass with singing not
with arithmetic
                    "a woman for me
         & a woman for thee" (he would order)
the one with a wen near her nipple
                    the other with a glass eye women
         with moist hair in their armpits
moister below
                    & furious
         reputed to be in love with great men they were
"nieces" to all the rabbis
                    breathless my demon would mount his
         from the rear the tsaddik
slept on in innocence of
                    heart & purpose
         barely
could feel her hand
                    betray him
         but blamed it on
the tightness of his linens while
                    wan allergic dreaming
         furry to his fingers
my demon
                    slept against the other's
         side forgetting
that the bride was always chaste the sabbath
                    always an interval
         between subscriptions
something cold but beautiful
                    not a mechanical process
         merely but responsive

to the touch

        in satin slippers beneath

    a painted canopy

of stars each waited

        for the bride

    each called her

sabbath but each had something else a different kind of sleep

        in mind

        (*coda*)

        once in a lifetime man

    may meet a hostile spirit once

he may be imprisoned for his

        dreams & pay for them

    lightning is like oil the motor

once it starts keeps

        running

    such was their wisdom though we had

no use for it

        only later seeing it

    reborn

in joplin on a billboard

        his own shadow

    was more than he could bear the war

came & he ran from it

        back in the cellar drinking

    too much he grew thin

the great encounter ended it

        in flames the candelabrum rose did it become

    a heart

that broke into sparks & letters

        a shower of ruined cities from which

    my demon

vanished fled from the light when I was born

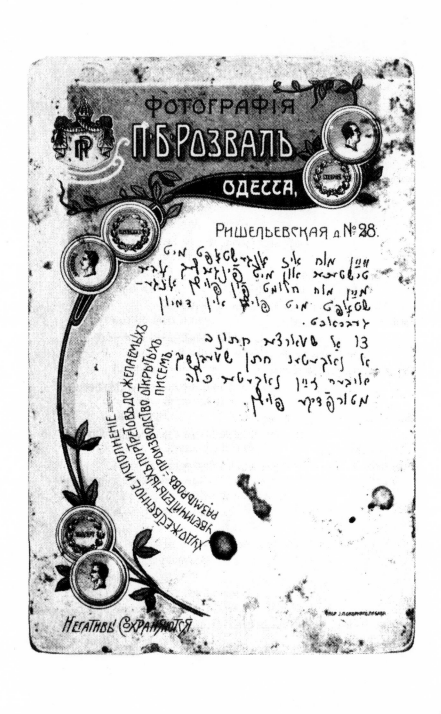

A BOOK OF WRITINGS

ANCESTRAL SCENES (I)

old crystal   a dry
piece of cake
remains
on the plate

          also herring scraps
          radishes
          slice of blackbread
          tea leaves
          etc.

  the man who farts
  likes it
  letting his muscles relax

  & feels inky
  more like a sponge than a man

how alarming, how
vulgar
they said, their way
of speaking

said it

ANCESTRAL SCENES (II)

> my grandfather's death
>
> was foolish
>
> he wiped his ass with
>
> > dirty newsprint
> >
> > died of blood poisoning in 1914
>
> had been a merchant
>
> > stationery
> >
> > wire thimbles
>
> glass beads
>
> > brooches
> >
> > "notions"
>
> a tray of cotton spools
>
> > he would find a chair
> >
> > piled high with
>
> cushions
>
> > broken springs
> >
> > where he could sleep
>
> dying
>
> > would dream of
> >
> > selling lemons
>
> yellow notebooks
>
> > the little
> >
> > stinking ends of jewish
>
> *vursht*

ANCESTRAL SCENES (III)

a small golden
snuffbox

>   otherwise
>   rabbinic collar
>   but open at the throat

>   a young man's beard
>   offsets
>   an old man's face

the first
electric bulb
lies splintered

"on a morning before the first world war
     electricity brought us lights"

mitzraim was only another name for egypt

>   salt in your eyes!
>   pepper in your nose!

ANCESTRAL SCENES (IV)

young boy standing on
a table
from his clothes hang
watches   jewelry
saffron-lidded eyes of his old grandfather
stare into his
between them start
processions of
pale jewish angels
throwing coins
that roll against the icing
of a cake
into which dough is traced
words of power
the picture of a fish
& many small holes
punched
into the surface
"therefore they called this cake a sieve"

AMULET

"Joseph
"is a fruitful bough
"a fruitful
"bough by eye of

"water
"branches who run over
"wall
"a wall runs

"over
"branches
"on the eye
"upon

A POLISH ANECDOTE   1931

"snuff too weak" you
soak in whiskey
you mix with fine pepper
your nose grows warm
& fat from it
you become a wealthy man
by sneezing
everybody says "god bless you"
the hairs inside your nose
grow hairs

A POLISH ANECDOTE   "Victory"

"he died among colleagues" runs
the Polish epitaph   the body
falls down from the saddle without
sorrow & the other soldiers

ride their horses over him singing
"sleep sleep dear colleague
"in your dark grave
"we wish you sweet dreams about Poland"

beautiful losses etc where each man
has many colleagues only one friend
said Marshal Pilsudski   "to be vanquished &
not to surrender   this is victory!"

A POLISH ANECDOTE   "The Saint"

the man who wouldn't kill an insect
scratched his balls
all day & half the night
would have the rabbi bless his pockets
smiled but never
at a woman   wouldn't even face his wife
but stared out the window
hands behind back he always placed
one foot before the other
remembering the saint who didn't know
his own wife had a wooden leg
until they buried her

A POLISH ANECDOTE   "The Banquet"

four serving spoons
in one dish of
fermented rye

barscz what greater
treat than this for
you   my children?

in a heavy
bowl or crock com—
bine flour &

boiling water
to a thick dough
let stand loosely

covered in a
warm spot in the
kitchen for at

least forty-eight
hours when the
dough begins to

rise add a quart
of cold water
let stand until

the liquid is
completely clear
to use remove

liquid without
stirring discard
when the dough be-

comes too slimey

A POLISH ANECDOTE   "The Sign"

she missed her period
hysteria
the rabbi said
& knew it!

wisemen generations
of sages
have walked before us
not tightlipped

not bachelors & fruitless
but wisemen!
could look at a woman
& say

she missed her period?
hysteria
the mole over her lip
a sign of grace

A POLISH ANECDOTE   "The Noble"

getting dead drunk he bled his jewish
barber with a shaky hand
or hiding from the cossacks still shouted
to the man who hid him
"take off your cap you jewish cunt"
a Radziwill can keep a boy's face
in a pail of water can make him
drink & puke then laugh at their women
forced to sit in trees crowing like
cocks would shower them with bullets
watch them fall & run but always
throw them coins or kiss another
Radziwill while mumbling
"beloved brother   go to hell!"

AMULET

"Black Striga
            black on black
"who eats black blood
                  & drinks it
"like an ox she bellows
"like a bear she growls
"like a wolf she crushes

THE NEOLITHIC DREAM OF RABBI NACHMAN

for Gary Snyder

a Jew so mad he heard the flowers
in the woods   singing
& understood each word
"them ice plants would've blowed your mind"

(says Rabbi Nachman) growing old
once slept inside a house
made of young trees   in dreams
he walked with the dead

& told his landlord
"you have killed these souls
"before their time
"but said no prayer for them

a poem for Rabbi Snyder

MORE VISIONS FROM THE NEOLITHIC RABBIS

for Nathaniel Tarn

first a steambath
then the men dived into
a muddy pool

water that smelled of
gasoline & sulphur
like all the pools in Beltz

that night they sang
"sweet love
"approach

"sweet love your bride
"is here
"o Bride o Sabbath Queen

& walked outside   saw
stars of Ukraine
were fat like oranges

a poem for Rabbi Tarn

A POEM FROM THE SAINT'S LIFE

his father called him a little flame
no no he was a blazing fire
he brought two mountaintops together
would carry a castle from the east
& set it in the king's yard
dreamy servants walked round the walls
bothered by the climate
they would confuse the meat & cheese
his dogs spoke hebrew   even
the birds wore prayershawls carried
rings in beaks
the names of God engraved in
amethyst   how tall
the saint grew

he started walking on a Friday
from Lodz to Mazowietz
managed to get there by the evening meal

AMULET

pishon	gihon	hiddekel	euphrates
nohsip	nohig	lekeddih	setarhpue
euphrates	hiddekel	gihon	pishon
setarhpue	lekeddih	nohig	nohsip
hiddekel	gihon	pishon	euphrates
lekeddih	nohig	nohsip	setarhpue
pishon	hiddekel	gihon	euphrates
nohsip	lekeddih	nohig	setarhpue

_____

The rivers of Paradise

From THE CODE OF JEWISH LAW

1
the worm because it
creeps you may not
eat of it   therefore

they threw out vinegar
& fruit they threw out
cereals or sifted them

with fish they searched
brains   intestines   liver
mouth & ears

round as a lentil were
those worms
some on their bodies

by their fins some
in their mouths
others beneath the gills

2
THE LOVERS

desired a partition
40" high

to block the light
not even moonlight

lit her body
lamplight

from another room
they shut out

with her fallen dress
& in the dark

wouldn't look between her legs
or kiss that place

in hunger
"to make yourselves detestable"

3
to let a rooster
wander

with a thread tied
to one leg

preventing it from
breaking dishes

but broke the law of rest
on saturdays

4
THE PROHIBITIONS

sowing   plowing   reaping   sheaving   threshing   winnowing
cleansing   crops   grinding   sifting   kneading   baking
shearing   blanching   carding   dyeing   spinning   weaving
making a minimum of two loops   weaving two threads   sep-
arating two threads   tying   untying   sewing a min-
imum of two stitches   ripping out in order to sew them
hunting a gazelle   slaughtering it   flaying it   salting
it   curing scraping or slicing its hide   writing a
minimum of two characters   erasing in order to write

them   building   wrecking   extinguishing   kindling
hammering   transporting

         & did not walk out with
         a needle   but only with a pin
         for clothes
         a watch became a burden
         though a silver key was more
         for show & eyeglasses
         wouldn't be carried not even
         in a silver frame
         "add no cloth to clothing for
         "the rain (they said)
         "unless against discomfort
         "a cane for lameness
         "but on the sabbath
         "the lame & the blind stay inside
         "with the chained man
         "others knowing that it's wrong to
         "walk on stilts through mud
         "& water   right
         "to wear a bandage of
         "poor cloth
         "& go out with cotton in your ear
         "or cotton wads against
         "a woman's
         "bleeding   not to
         "spare her clothes but
         "give her comfort
         "a man may wear two coats if one
         "is for a friend
         "likewise two pairs of slippers
         "two hats
         "two belts   also (they said)

"avoid a rope with two
"knots in it to hold
"your pants up   take off all
"suspenders
"& put no handkerchief
"around thy neck
"or leg
"no gloves on thy hands
"but wear
"a toupee on thy head
"of flax or wool
"the woman who holds
"an eagle-stone
"against miscarriage may
"still walk freely
"on the sabbath

5
circumcision
at a graveside

they give the child
a name

but pronounce no
benediction

to cut off
that disgrace

6

don't eat the blood
in eggs   (she said)
the blood in fish wd satisfy her
but don't serve it gathered
in a vessel fearing
people wd talk she also feared
biting a crust of break wd crack
her gums & draw blood in
she wd later cut away   wd watch
for blood in milk
particles of meat between her teeth
of cheese on table she ate meat from
rinsed her mouth   swept her tablecloth
& baking goat in milk-of-almonds
wd put whole almonds in
fearing people wd see the whiteness & wd talk

7

going from darkness to
a well-lit room
opened the door a crack

looked at a little light
then eased it further
& walked in

because the sun is gradual
he was   & feared it
in reflection

wdn't have windows facing north
even so wanted
a sky without obstructions

didn't read at dusk but not
at midday either
avoided staring at anything

too white   but red
cd hurt him also   smoke could
or fine dust against his eyes

sulphurous odors
strong wind blowing in his face
excessive breathing   tears

"my eyes do fail with tears"
but more with too much fucking
"the precept of the lord is pure

"enlightening the eyes"

8
a dangerous proposition   fish
& meat together
even if it's chickenfat
but water
between courses helps
wash the food down   rinse the mouth
& sweat a problem
too   a poison
really   not the face's
sweat I mean the body's therefore
he never put food
under his clothes he never
bit coins that sweat

had clung to   he was very clean
if spit formed in his mouth
while smelling food
he never swallowed it avoiding
danger to his body

9

THE ENCHANTMENTS

he said the bread dropped from his mouth
the cane fell from his hand
his son called him from behind

a raven croaked at him
a deer crossed his path
a snake passed on his right

a fox passed on his left
& ruined his journey
as a bird's singing might

he said he couldn't pay
it was too early
he said it was the sabbath

the new moon frightened him he said
the hen should die for crowing
like a cock & meant: the hen should die

10
your hands are full of blood
because you think of it
& touch it
you make it hard by
sleeping on it
or leaning up against a friend
or watching animals & birds die
even by riding horseback
or holding it while pissing
or soaping it
or wearing your pants too tight
or reading books by gentiles
or eating fatty foods
or by not eating fatty foods
but turning over in your sleep
& farting in a cold bed
the milk from your own body
running down your leg
staining the sheets with dishonor
yellow & stiff
by morning
that has made you a murderer
someday will raise
the midnight lament for
the temple   demanding
repentance to hold
the circumcised babe by its leg
smile at the iron-toothed mother
but turn from the shame of
your flesh   in love
& the pursuit of peace

AMULET

master	occupied	sang	under
of	shadows	drove	ritual
dreams	the	breath	fringes
led	moon	further	like
his	dancers	down	letters
party	trembled	it	his
marched	beautiful	emerged	name
to	men	in	shapes
volhynian	lifted	red	22
woods	gowns	cloud	verbs

TREE SPIRIT EVENTS (Zohar)

Then sing the trees of the wood for joy
before the Lord.

One mounts to one side.
One descends on that side.
One enters between the two.
Two crown themselves with a third.
Three enter into one.
One produces various colors.
Six of them descend on one side & six of them on the other.
Six enter into twelve.
Twelve bestir themselves to form twenty-two.
Six are comprised in ten.
Ten are fixed in one.

ALPHABET EVENT (1)

Recite the 221 alphabets while walking in a circle.
Repeat the event 442 times.

ALPHABET EVENT (2)

Do the first Alphabet Event walking backwards.
Recite the alphabets starting from the end.

> *And I walked by his side & he took me by his hand & raised me upon his wings & showed me those letters, all of them, that are graven with a flaming sword on the throne of glory: And sparks go forth from them & cover all the chambers of 'Araboth.*

WORD EVENT

He sits in a house whose walls are decorated with fresh vegetables, praying & singing psalms, & reading from *The Book of Law*.

Then he begins to move the letters that he sees, until they make new words & sounds.

Quickly he jumps from word to word, letting the words form thoughts in any order.

Finally be drops the words out of his mind: word by word until he thinks of nothing.

Freed from thought, the consonants dance around him in quick mtion. Forming a mirror in which he sees his face.

BOOK EVENT

Bring an old book to a cemetery & bury it.

WOMAN'S EVENT (I)

A woman washes face & hands in water mixed with the sap of an apple tree.

WOMAN'S EVENT (2)

At the foot of a fruit tree a woman buries a bowl filled with menstrual blood.

WOMAN'S EVENT (3)

A woman crawls under the belly of a pregnant mare.

WOMAN'S EVENT (4)

A woman strokes the limbs of a bride or bridegroom.

WOMAN'S EVENT (5)

A woman drinks a mixture of wild tea leaves, or a woman eats a rooster complete with comb & gizzard, or a woman drinks water seeped in the ashes of a burnt male rabbit.

WOMAN'S EVENT (6)

A woman swallows the foreskin of a newly circumcised infant.

THE NUMBERS (1)

Then did the Master read the text: All sevens are beloved.

Then he said: Take seven prickles from seven palm trees, seven chips from seven beams, seven nails from seven bridges, seven ashes from seven ovens, seven scoops of earth from seven door-sockets, seven pieces of pitch from seven ships, seven handfuls of cumin, & seven hairs from the beard of an old dog, & tie them to the neckhole of the shirt with a white twisted cord.

And Again:
4 lamps
4 ladders
4 children of the flowers of the priesthood
shook 4 willow branches
toward the 4 directions

THE NUMBERS (2)

She wears
pearls.
Makes a bag of black velvet
for her husband
& a gold star.
She adds honey to his milk.
He asks for raisins
& cherry juice.
His coat is made of fox fur.
Barefoot
they go running.
Seven.
Seven.
Seven.
Seven.
Seven.
Four.

She waves a goosewing
duster.
They drink brandy from tin mugs.
Carp's head
wrapped in cabbage leaves
for dinner.
He buys a strip of licorice from a Turk.
She wears a beaded jacket.
He smokes a long pipe with an amber mouthpiece.
She smokes sweet-smelling cigarettes.
Seven.

Seven.
Seven.
Seven.
Seven.
Four.

Her shoes are pointed.
His shoes are sometimes made of straw.
Sometimes he drinks from a red-painted glass.
She washes her breasts with rainwater.
Four.

Four.
Four.
Four.
Four.
Four.
Four.
Four.
Seven.

He wears a thirteen-pointed hat
edged with skunk.
The letters he draws look like mountains.
His wife writes Hebrew like a man.
He makes her repeat the names of angels.
Four.

Four.
Four.
Four.
Four.
Four.

Four.
Four.
Seven.

She pulls the longboots
off his feet.
The sound of gramophones
comes through their windows.
She walks on her hands.
He taps on her shutters with
his wooden hammer.
His chairs turn over
his dishes break.
Later he stops the clock.
Her eyes are different
colors.
Seven.

Seven.
Seven.
Seven.
Seven.
Four.

He carries a snuffbox made of bone.
A silver pouch holds his tobacco.
She chews on a coin with her gold teeth.
He tells her to let the boiled milk form a skin.
Four.

Four.
Four.
Four.

Four.
Four.
Four.
Four.
Seven.

Hot peppered peas under
a mass of rags.
Squab & egg noodles for dinner.
His pitchblack beard with its two points.
Cow bladders in place of
windows.
Hands in a tub of yellow dough.
A trace of hair on the Queen's feet.
The smile of a man who speaks pure German.
Seven.

Seven.
Seven.
Seven.
Seven.
Four.

"SHE"

1
She Shekinah
She Kingship
She Dwelling

She Daughter
She Lady
She Pearl

She Precious
She Cornerstone
She Female

She Floweth
She Male
She Garden

She Garment
She Earth
She Ocean

She Omen
She Lady of Light
She Sarah

She Slave
She Sucketh the Gods
She Rebekkah

She Rachel
She Leah
She Moon with the Hair

She the Hoverer

2
She Matronit
She Dancer
She Northerner

She in the Night
She Agrath
She Igrath

She Ishtar
She Tail of the Comet
She Child

She Charmer
She Crooked
She Serpent

She Stiff Necked
She Stick
She Lilith

She Liar
She Thorn
She Screech Owl

She Stranger
She Alien Crown
She Heaven

She Howler
She Hole
She the Hole for the Dead

She Dazzler

AMULET

אבג יתץ קרע שטן נגד יכש בטר צתג...
ל פזק שקוצית בשכמלו בשם שדי יוי
לילית
אביטי אביזו
אמרוסו הקש אודם
איק פודו אייל ומטרוסה
אבנ קסה שטרוגה קלי
בטוח חיל י פריט
סהש

YOU'VE HEARD HER ON THE RADIO, SEEN HER ON T.V.
NOW SEE HER IN HER OWN HOME

MME. SHEKINAH

JEWISH SOUL
HEALER & ADVISER

Removes Evil Spirits
and Bad Luck from your home

Wh at your eyes will see
Your heart will believe

Guaranteed to Help in 3 Days

She will tell you what you want to know, give figures
and facts of business matters, love, health family
affairs. if the one you love is true or false. What part
of country is luckiest and what to do to be successfull.
Has helped thosands from all walks of life and can
help you too. Bring your problems to her. She will
help you solve them.

I do solemnly swear to make no charge if I don't
faithfully fulfill every word in this statement and tell
you what you want to know about friends, enemies or
rivals, whether your husband, wife or sweetheart is
true or false; how to gain the love of the one you
desire; control or influence the action of anyone even
though miles away. I further guarantee & promise to
make no charge unless you find me superior to any
reader you've consulted. I succeed where others fail
☞ Readings in Reach of All HALF PRICE with this ad.

Mrs. L. L. nee E.K, 10 Attorney St. one flt up **N.Y.C.**
open daily & Sun. 8a.m. - 9p.m. Tel. POland 0 - 1931

GALICIAN NIGHTS,
OR A NOVEL IN PROGRESS

GALICIAN NIGHTS, OR A NOVEL IN PROGRESS

The Early Life, Loves & Circumstances of Esther K.

1

Because a Jew eats meat & grows fat he waits until he sees the Governor.

The Jew's beard is sleek, so are his eyes sleek & shameless in an otherwise bland face.

Greetings, says Jew to Governor, but the Governor doesn't respond, no he stands there smiling.

At once the Jew gives him a fat portion & draws back.

Ah, says the Governor in awe. His fingers dip into the dish, dip & are lost.

Does the Jew withdraw then?

No.

Does the Governor return to purge his land of Jews?

No. the Governor doesn't return nor does he purge his land.

What does he do then?

He trembles on the balance of a kiss, he dawdles, he grows sick, he waves his arms, he vanishes, he is heard of nevermore.

2

He trembles on the balance of a kiss, he dawdles, he grows sick, he waves his arms, he vanishes, he is heard of nevermore.

The Governor is lost, she says, says it & goes inside the house.

The cart standing in her studio is the same one they rode around the town.

My love! cries Esther K. as she undresses.

Sometimes he rushes from her room, naked himself & with a sock around his forehead.

Reddish eyelids, yellow melancholy eyes, he was her gentile, she called him "little goy."

Now she puts snuff in both her nostrils.

It is evening. It is 1931 in Poland. It is better to be naked. It is more than that. It is worth it. Is it? It is too soon. It is noon. It is like early November it is really June.

And Esther K. is bathing.

Greet the Governor for me, winks Esther K., & rubs the soap between her thighs.

Her gold tooth glitters.

The mirror swings along its golden chain. He is dreaming again of gold utensils.

A little to the left, a little shy, a little heavy in his socks, a little wet, a little like her father, a little less, a little lonely.

If you sneeze, he says & turns aside.

I love you.

What a dove is Esther K.!

3

And what a dove is born to Esther K.!

Greetings remarketh the Governor.

They have come in procession to bless the child of her flesh, the midwife removeth it as one removeth a thorn.

A white-haired child which smelleth of old laundry.

Soon Esther K. ariseth from her bed red ribbons around her leg & bangeth the door shut.

(This was in fulfillment of her dream.)

She cutteth the navel string & putteth a grain of salt beneath the infant's tongue. She rubbeth white honey upon her lips, also upon his arms.

They drop a honeycomb into his cradle.

Will Esther K. see the produce of her womb beyond this morning?

Perhaps so perhaps no, says Esther K. & sings *O little golden one sleep in thy cradle*, her own first song.

Galician nights, how beautiful & how lonely.

But for the Jewess who has tasted of the Gentiles' honey there is no reunion in her father's tent

no awning of white satin no wedding knives no tribal beard to hide her face beneath.

O Esther K. thou my semitic beauty thou easter excellence

thou poor foresaken witness yet plyest thy trade in peace!

Thou warmest a towel for the Governor.

Thou wearest a rose gown.

(A man, once come on business, learneth to stay & bathe with thee.)

Thou eatest tripe & poppy seeds.

Thou sharest half thy bounty with the rich.

4

Esther K. receives a letter from China. It reads:

Darling Esther K.

This is a wonderful Chinese city & there is here also a wonderful Jewish community. The center of the life of the community is its remarkable synagogue which is reputed to be very ancient. The community itself is said also to be very ancient & to go perhaps back to the lost tribe of Asher, one of the famous ten lost tribes of Israel. Isaiah the Prophet speaks of Jews who had settled in the land of the

Sinim, but be that as it may it is certain that from the 7th century on, Persian Jews were coming into China by way of India. There are today four thousand Jews in China whose appearance is not to be distinguished from that of the Chinese. But don't let that fool you since they all play Mah Jong according to the Ashkenazic variation so familiar to us & not the rather simpler native form. There is also in the city a good theater, several western-style beauty parlors & at least one kosher restaurant managed by a family of Russian exiles. Charity abounds here. The Sisterhood flourishes. The study of the Law, while not brilliant, is steady, & at least it imposes few new burdens. The climate is "ideal."

In addition a wonderful man resides here whom you would love to meet. While I cannot divulge his name I am at liberty to inform you that his initials are L.L. A trip to this corner of the Diaspora will truly change your life.

(N.B. When you have finished reading this letter make six copies & sign your name to each, then remit them to six of your dearest friends. You must do this within three days of receipt or disastrous consequences will follow; if you comply however the results will bring you instantaneous good luck. (Holofernes failed to comply & was beheaded by Judith: Count Potocki complied & was spared to meet God as a martyr.))

It is a serious matter, dearest, & a sure sign of the coming triumph of the Lord's Anointed!

The letter bears a lion in the lower corner
& a sacred lemon.
There is otherwise no signature.

5

Circumstances in a Jewish house.

Circumstances of Esther K.

Circumstances of men exchanging wallets in front of the guild-hall.

Circumstances of carts circumstances of leather lines in the hands of the master drivers.

Circumstances of farewells. Of parades of gymnasts on the road to Warsaw.

Circumstances of Bialystok & what lay beyond.

Circumstances of buttons circumstances of sewing each thread into place not leaving the ends untied.

Circumstances of half-understood lines in three rhyming poems by distinctively different Yiddish poets.

Circumstances in a Jewish house.

Circumstances of "gypsy costumes & Polish happenings in the woods."

Circumstances of chance meetings in the market.

Gentile circumstances & circumstances filled with danger.

Circumstances of letters written under cover of night.

Circumstances of the beautiful rape.

(Some circumstances that were easy others that brought great riches.

Circumstances & insurance.)

Circumstances of Esther K.

Circumstances of the journey Esther K. took across the ocean.

Circumstances of her noble station on Attorney Street.

Circumstances of the queen among the Persians the Governor is kind to her she bites his beard.

Circumstances of the 7:10 to Warsaw & the 8:35 to Babylon.

Circumstances of better times when will we come on better times again?

Circumstances of Esther K. & China.

Circumstances of Jews in pigtails & of a visit by the false messiah Leo Levy.

Circumstances of his dream of Shabtai Tswi's dream of a Turkish heaven.

Circumstances of the Shekinah leaning on his arm.

Circumstances of the Shekinah with twelve breasts & of her lover with only two hands to caress them.

Circumstances of the Shekinah in a sea of milk.

Circumstances of her return to Poland.

(O Poland of the saints unbuttoned Poland repeating endlessly the triple names of Mary.)

Circumstances of King Casimir & the Jewish queen who sat beside him.

Circumstances of a Kazar kingdom ruled by women.

Circumstances of a golden foreskin.

Circumstances of the monarch strangled by a silky rope then buried in Paradise with forty others.

Circumstances of the legends I never knew that were kept from me in childhood.

Circumstances of her mind & ours.

Circumstances of her own face appearing in the Polish rotogravure (a decade later in the Denver Post).

Circumstances of smoked mackerel.

Circumstances of her mother's hands around a goose's neck. Of hers around the fatmeat of the King of Poland.

Circumstances of heaven circumstances of halvah circumstances of half a loaf.

(I have brought you these circumstances toward a tale of Esther K.)

Circumstances of Galician nights circumstances on the road to Warsaw & on Attorney Street.

Circumstances in Persia China & the Kazar Kingdom.

Circumstances of the cost of milk & honey.

Circumstances in a Jewish house.

Circumstances of the loves of Esther K.

A Morning in the Life of Mister Leo Levy

1

He went to sleep in Jewishtown woke up early the next morning feeling how forlorn it was to be lost & foundering from three directions.

The demon was gone, gone too the bench but not misst.

(His own was too long for comfort.)

(Too much of a secret.)

He waked between rooms a separate landscape coming to life in each hand.

Elijah!

As his name beckoned his eye would surge past extremities the remembered morning's socks buried in each boot he had to dig his hand into & couldn't bear it.

He sighed then, one short *oy* for each long *vey* & several *ays* (eyes) (I's) along the edges, let them hear him if they minded or touch the pasty cloth in place of.

Pheh.

The leather had natural holes to it washed by several months of russias snowfalls polands muds pebbled water by the black sea pricked by thorns of bukavina dungedup roads of hungary sizzledover fires drafty synagogues were-full-of scorched & cracked like holy relics.

(*Oy!*)

So saying he has turned himself away his legs drawn in against his chest (he coughs & makes them tremble) in a rage with life.

2

But his longcoat (black) was on a large chair (yellow) in which a lion (red) was carved, the letters *lamed beth yod hey* above it like his own name Leo Levy not the name he used in his profession but reminded of it always anyhow when seeing that symbol of old powers the exile kept alive.

A lion by birth a liar later, hah!

He hated tea less than he loved money so had to be stuck with the taste of it.

A lemon.

The pulp had turned brown with the night's passing, more dirt & corruption to contend with. Brown of piss in pot. Why had he brought his powers to this place. A pox no a cholera on it!

Contagion.

This comes from being a jew.

The doctors (victims themselves) had no name for it.

One, who was preeminent among his fellows, came to the house (it was the week of tabernacles) & prescribed immediate retirement.

His health was dependent on it, his home so far away. The doctor had to be brought into his confidence (& was!) before there was any hope for a return to his senses.

Why blackbread? he was asked.

Why onions?

Why break the bread into small pieces & cut the onion rings with the middle fingernail & thumbnail?

He had been going at it wrong & had made himself sicker.

There was little hope now.

Less for those who sat around him in the bathhouse.

Would he tell them beautiful stories of his youth in Fairbanks?

Yes he had the fingers of a jeweler.

Yes one eye was blue.

3

The other eye was impossible to know any longer, though one would guess it the same color as its still present member.

Yet since nothing is certain (thus was it written in the Talmud where it was also written that everything would be known) you could hardly argue from the glass back to the jelly.

The glass was green.

Sovereign pickles floated in a tub of brine, they were the first sight after his long surgery

mirrored in the green eye too they trembled in the blue one like the gnarled moist fingers of a manyhanded idol.

Will she recognize me when we meet again or I her now that the world is flattened in my sight?

Her buxomness, her boobs I frankly sucked, her plums her bosoms her delights her apertures her jellied (gelid) roundness.

Flat? *Drat!*

He rips it from its socket then hurls it with a *zets* against the wall.

4

Oy what a carnage was what lamentations were.

This is the angry song that Leo Levy made for Esther K.:

Angry Song

I hate Esther K. because I am ugly

I hate Esther K. & am angry at her because I am ugly

I hate Esther K. & am angry at her contempt for me because I am ugly

I hate Esther K. & am angry at her contempt for me which I deserve less than she knows because I am ugly

I hate Esther K. & am angry at her contempt for me which I deserve less than she knows being estranged from me because I am ugly

I hate Esther K. & am angry at her contempt for me which I deserve less than she knows being estranged from me who went to sleep in Jewishtown because I am ugly

I hate Esther K. & am angry at her contempt for me which I deserve less than she knows being estranged from me who went to sleep in Jewishtown I feel so sad because I am ugly

I hate Esther K. & am angry at her contempt for me which I deserve less than she knows being estranged from me who went to sleep in Jewishtown I feel so sad to be a fornicator of demons because I am ugly

I hate Esther K. & am angry at her contempt for me which I deserve less than she knows being estranged from me who went to sleep in Jewishtown I feel so sad to be a fornicator of demons & to smell of onions because I am ugly

I hate Esther K. & am angry at her contempt for me which I deserve less than she knows being estranged from me who went to sleep in Jewishtown I feel so sad to be a fornicator of demons & to smell of onions & to see God's pickles with my true blue eye because I am ugly

I hate Esther K. & am angry at her contempt for me which I deserve less than she knows being estranged from me who went to sleep in Jewishtown I feel so sad to be a fornicator of demons & to smell of onions & to see God's pickles with my true blue eye & nothing with my lovely glass eye because I am ugly

I hate Esther K. & am angry at her contempt for me which I deserve

less than she knows being estranged from me who went to sleep
in Jewishtown I feel so sad to be a fornicator of demons & to
smell of onions & to see God's pickles with my true blue eye &
nothing with my lovely glass eye no this is no way to treat the
Lord's anointed because I am ugly

OY OY OY IT'S HARD TO BE A JEW!

THE SEVEN MELODIES OF ESTHER K.

1
The pink head of her father
under a black skullcap.
Radishes.

2
Will you visit us up the stairs.
(I had climbed there already.)
We sat in a circle of worshippers.
He said   My name is Leo Levy.
(I loved the name.)
& his hair reached down to his shoulders.
Comb it comb it
he cried.
(I took the comb &
jammed it down.
Electricity ran from his beard.)

3

Did Jews learn to smile?
they asked him.
His answer was "once"
"maybe" came easy to his lips
it was a way
of smiling   serious   amused
& with a smile.

4

A marriage to the Jewish king.
& a Chinese holiday.
Good fortune.
Clear sailing.
Bright days.
Happiness is just around the corner.

5

Ride on my white leopard.
(Give me a boost.)
He said yes.
(Can I stand on your shoulders.)
Only if you promise not to fall.
(I do.)
There's Jerusalem.
(You can't come into Jerusalem on a leopard.)
Then on what.
(A rickshaw pulled by goats.)
No a chariot.
(Then a chariot pulled by leopards.)
No by donkeys.
(You can't come into Jerusalem on a donkey.)

6

In love with a gypsy
how beautiful
my days are   my feet
begin in Vilna
& carry me to Havana.
He rubs my pudenda
& buys me a manicure.
I will follow his motorcycle
up the Great Wall of China.

7

Two hundred & forty-eight parts of her body.
Three hundred & sixty-five veins.

VARIATION ON A JEWISH LOVE SONG
(The Sixth Melody of Esther K.)

In love with a gypsy
how beautiful
my days are   my feet
begin in Vilna
& carry me to Havana.
He rubs my pudenda
& stuffs it with his frankfurter.
I will follow his motorcycle
up the Great Wall of China.

ISAAC LURIA'S "HYMN TO SHEKINAH FOR THE FEAST OF THE
SABBATH" NEWLY SET ROSH HASHONAH 5733
BY JEROME ROTHENBERG

I have sung
an old measure

would open
gates to

her field of apples
(each one a power)

set a new table
to feed her

& beautifully
candelabrum

drops its
light on us

Between right & left
the Bride

draws near in
holy jewels

clothes of the sabbath
whose lover

embraces her
down to foundation

gives pleasure
squeezes his strength out

in surcease of
sorrow

& makes new faces
be hers

& new souls
new breath

gives her joy
double measure

of lights & of
streams for her blessing

o Friends of the Bride
go forth

give her many
sweet foods to taste

many kinds of
fish

for fertility
birth

of new souls
new spirits

will follow the 32 paths
& 3 branches

the bride with
70 crowns

with her King who
hovers above her

crown above crown in
Holy of Holies

this lady all worlds are
formed in

all's sealed
within her

shines out from
Ancient of Days

Toward the south
I placed

candelabrum
(o mystical)

room in
the north

for table
for bread

for pitchers of wine
for sweet myrtle

gives power to
lovers

new potencies
garlands

of words for her
70 crowns

50 gates
the Shekinah

ringed by
6 loaves

of the sabbath
& bound

all sides to
Heavenly Refuge

the hostile
powers

have left us
demons you feared

sleep in chains

ESTHER K. COMES TO AMERICA

POLAND/1931 "A Gallery of Jews"

a gallery of Jews, love
so perfect it becomes
a solid thing   a person's
or a monster's face made of candles
"if we could only hold the lips
in place" the pink flesh
falls   how beautiful & old
(the women sing) this is no graven image
it is the body of your father
sleeping he was young
he would only wake up to read a book
or smell the rolls
baking in the oven his sisters
cared for
others were walking
in the woods still others
had vanished among the Gentiles
young girls in neckties
riding horses some would buy
magazines with pictures of Polish cities
some wrote to Paris or U.S.A.
& wouldn't eat
Sundays were spent in groups
girls held each other
but spoke of lovers
from the towns   even the young men
sitting on each other's laps

dreamed freedom
on distant walls the wax
was running down
like tears their mothers
wept on Fridays
while waiting for the meat & prunes
still in love
the sisters fitted neatly
into the picture of the perfect town
the young men left for Cuba
farewells
not blessings followed
where they went
the sun was always going down
& shifted
one made a movie   he would dance
his way through life
forgetting his mother's baldness
the virtues that made a woman strong
he fell in love with Gentiles
real blondes were always on his lawn
speaking in German
he would strip down & ride them
psalms burst from his throat
"honkeytonk joys" delivered in a mock accent
he flew westward
to California   no one
wore corsets now
though some forgot how to smile
others would praise him for his teeth
his eyes were ageless
like his clothes
only the pockets changed
the papers faded
walking on country roads at night

still holding hands
the women kept heading toward the towns
old friends had died
along the way to   she could tell you
the exact location of each grave
minutes added up
they would be charged for them in dollars
growing poorer
someone would shuffle the cards
but no one was playing
the photos had slipped into her lap
her glasses fogged
the miracle was that the candle
could keep burning
that there was no one
holding it above his head
to let the wax drip down
the wax had gathered in a metal dish
yellow & pink it sputtered
in the candle's light

THE IMMIGRANT

for Charles Chaplin

feathers hang from the fingers of the immigrant
who will embrace an egg   whose eyelids
even now close over the first half-dollar in the world
a moon for the desert America was building
suddenly gone haywire falling soft & cheezey
down an endless line of streets with restaurants
polished floors you slid on as the waiter
the electrician sometimes even sometimes

the man who finds a stranger's wallet
in his soup   runs off from there
to Yellowstone poor epileptic honeymooner
who wears a bearcoat in the Rockies
your bear-love licking at your trail
far from Newark desperado with a rubber gun
you make your final shootout with the bearded lawmen
but earlier the week you rode in steerage
Rotterdam receded only the smell of sausages
brought Poland back that and the message
of the unwashed cunt the lady in the bunk above you
aimed at your nose bright sexual pickles
a garlic polka with all the words changed into Yiddish
the Hungarian tenor intercepted slipping
a hand into her drawers then left you
seated on a stoop in Monroe Street an orphan
inattentive to the band that played The Immigrant Shuffle
you learned to labor slowly
at first but tested your dreams of leisure
in the bitter factories the dark Jew
was your boss the bright Jewess
worked beside you on the line
would fill your dinnerpail with stuffed dough
chickpeas incredible farmer cheeses wrapped in rags
tastes that lit up names in your mind
from the old town   of girls with poppyseed eyes
smiles of white raisins
whose mouths still moist from puddings
encircled your putz their heavy
honeydew breasts cut open licked clean
later in your secular imagination
sleeping with the German collie you attempted
abominations to the rabbis hugged the gentle fur
in friendship your first drop of semen
freed you   maddened   into cabarets

to sing the song scrawled on your shirtsleeve
the words in middle European ageless anthem of your race
no demoralized proletarian you were
the sweet soul in exile cockeyed scholar
who couldn't spell his name but stood
three hours in long underwear (torn in back to show
a handsome pair of balls) outside the steamroom
devised a fancy maneuver to keep a step
ahead of the Sicilian faggot with raised bathbrush
twirling his heavy moustaches soaked in pepper
gaily you put your lips to his then sneezed him
through the doorway   falling   saw his cruel life
snuffed under the feet of marchers
strikers you led down Easy Street & up into Heaven
became an Irish cop yourself but kept your earlocks
your gaberdines hidden you still ate radishes for lunch
scraps of chickenwings for dinner let the skin
slide down your throat & choke you
the contradictions were almost a relief
for some for you the clock kept spinning
wheels hummed in the tower
everything ran by electricity & worried you
nickels & dimes sparked into life they bounced
off counters into your cuffs now you were always bending
looking at your shoes would even stick chewing gum
on broomsticks sought lost gold down manholes
from there you took the steamer
to Alaska trudged endless miles from Fairbanks
with your Yukon love   howling   you wore a derby
suspenders pulled your pants up to your chest
& left you gasping   visions from last year's snowstorms
filled your eyes & mind with gold
gold were your watch & chain your teeth were gold
you walked on a gold carpet America was gold to you
a gold boat drifted on a lake of gold

in the cabin gold men sat around a table
their smiles were gold & frozen like the gold fly
halfway between the ceiling & the floor
suspended in your dream of gold
becomes a gold pin for your tie the golden girl clips off
will let you stroke a gold tit in return
she smiles for the demonic newsmen
flashbulbs shatter the limits of your wakefulness
at midday   in forfeit of all love

ESTHER K. COMES TO AMERICA: 1931

The Wilderness: but otherwise
name of a cafeteria
where the two lovers drink tea
not speaking to each other
but sharing a world through separation:
1931: Esther K.
& Leo Levy
have met here at the end of a short life:
nothing begins as painfully
as the first step outside the glass door
the first sight of traffic
even the rumblings of the new subway under Houston Street:
all this happened in the course of ages
the priest tormented her & that was one
the governor broke into sighs & that was another
her mother became incontinent & that was the third
other events followed: fourth was the birth
of a child dead at childbirth
she massaged its hands but had to suck her own breasts:

stale odors: Leo Levy
going every morning to the chicken market
pursues his dream of power
Esther K. wonders: how was I ever trapped
inside this body?
in another life she would have been
a playgirl: not she
but someone else threw roses
in the Dnieper
danced on the drifting ice floe
to America
not someone else but she
opened the fly of the Shanghai dog-merchant
& greased his cock:
flesh erupting in the tropics
bewildering parrots
bathed in the mind of Esther K.
the traveler who crossed the Ganges
found Harlem
on the other side
the man with six fingers on one hand
had four on the other:
thus history repeated itself with marked rapidity
leading her to first meet
& then lose
Leo Levy: leading him
to polish his fingernails
with eggwhite
leading them both to read fortunes in earwax
to sell candy in Turkish baths
& cotton in Canada
to remake "1931" as a talking movie:
what lovely dreams the world will have of Esther K.
said Leo Levy
I will make dreams for the world to have of Esther K.

& garments to wear in her image
I will comb her hair out until it reaches to Nicaragua
then will climb its length
& let it carry me to the top of a windy boat
sailing for Jerusalem: farewell!
the next price of almonds is a fair price
the poor under your window & the poor
around your table
will always be there: the bicyclists will too
but peddling backwards stumbling
against churches they will pretend
to drop behind: a crisis
the good life of the timid
beckons: it is a value
to be learned: a source of fortune
only too distant without refinement
both will grow sick & die
much later: separate beds
wait for them
chimeras dressed as chorus girls
to direct & love: his name
changed to Ben Messiah
hers to his: an aged couple
smelling of wet sheets
they will sometimes be holding hands
feeling how small the palms are: the Wilderness
has shrunk them: tomorrow
morning
was a lie:
a glass of tea:
maybe a bun with onions:
a suck:
two bitter almonds:
three half-chewed jelly slices:
a lemon

a lemon
a lemon
a lemon
a lemon
a lemon
etc.

POLAND /1931   "The Paradise of Labor"

an inheritance   hardly dreamed of
they had carried it with them into the new city
during a time of ice Christmas mad December
pictures of their mothers covered the walls deep frames
held light in the corners under glass
he spoke with Gentiles more often these days working
the tops of shoes he dreamed of organizations
marched on Maydays from opposite ends of the town
the young men had come into another world
children with dogs & cats
sat on the high stoops some carved wood
others threw rocks at birds
waiting with mud between their toes they whistled
"the paradise of labor" was their song
a big round-bellied samovar hummed on the table
music was everywhere the walls were dancing
the cigarettes were English & smelled sweet to them
at night the young men slept together
not partners yet they were comrades
to each other   each left a sister
in their little town each shaved his head
& wore short jackets

dreamed past the Pripet Marshes to the Russian meadows
cities of pamphleteers
boulevards of orators
mechanics skilled in languages
& economics
naked proletarians in the woods of middle Europe
flowers with a single name
he brought back to his bed at night
walking from the shop the workers studyhouse
a comrade threw an arm around him
in the half light of blankets
he saw the ankle tighten something
like a web between the toes
his fingers pushed through his own hair
pulled back
he read his misfortune in the other's eyes
the evil urge their fathers
had called it   laughter in alleyways
battalions of pimps & thieves
invaded their classrooms stole all the girls
& shipped them to degradation
in Buenos Aires   only the young men
remained a hot breath
bothered his shoulder
the vision exploded into other rooms
comrades in a solitary dance
hasidic & lonely
circled the red-painted floor
the music slowed down freeing
the words to race ahead
the Great Name of God in his throat
choked him a stocking with hot salt
around his neck
his mother's lips touched his forehead again

carried in her apron kneaded
into her dough he sat
in the dust of an abandoned synagogue
a shoebox on his head
pendant of garlic cloves down to his waist
& a dead goose
he held a herring-head in one hand
an almsbox in the other
grandfathers walked over him & spat in his face
the international movement
trembled ranks broke
Lenin's beard floated on the Dnieper
torn from the dreamer his underwear
flew like a flag from the Tsar's palace
the young men were holding hands seated
on both sides of a long
table no a long bed
in uniforms with earlocks
still curled watching
the grandfather cut the bread of abundance
but hatless   telling them
"I am Karl Marx come to bring you to Paradise
"place the kiss on thy brother's lips in Paradise   red
"replica of the matriarchy's love for her children"
a veil
a kerchief over the head of their mother
(hairless)
the young men find no love in their bodies
but are always hopeful
tomorrow brings each one a small store
marriage the promise of revolution
the scientific study of history etcetera
into the snow of Poland he walks
as a straggler he comes down the center

of the road   on either side
rows of hooded men saintly processions
of workers to whom he speaks
in Yiddish
like an oriental Christ

THE MURDER INC. SUTRA

for Robert Kelly

Pincus Tavern
which Kelly passed
as schoolboy   den
of murderers or den of Jews
as murderers
no Benya Kriks he says
but bad guys simply
rotten
in the way America
disposes   though I pretend
other Pincus Taverns meetingplaces of one-eyed
hand in caftan hardcocked
Jewish bandits
beautiful men of noses enlarged with purple veins
of still-curled earlocks from childhood
who dared to cross the border in three coats
watchbands laid out from wrist to shoulders
but beardless could whistle
lost messages in secret Jewish code
meaning
"the Tsar's asshole smells of vinegar" etcetera
& were obliged to wield knives   not only

to cut a notch off a salami
but slit a windpipe
spreading his blood across
the merchant's vest or seeing
pictures in it
of rabbis with hardons unheard of
in the secular world
real to their perceptions who were
brothel Jews & inn-
keepers
expert in management of taverns
where most would let the Polacks
drink but took a piece
themselves if pressed to it
even would suck each other off
in Polish prisons
from there to Brooklyn emanations
made the journey   sought
Golden Kingdoms
at the corner of Stone & Sutter
(Kelly thought) some lounged
in doorways   improbable murderous Litvaks
with names like Lepke   Gurrah   "Dutch Schultz"
      Rothstein   Lansky   Siegel
would drive wing'd cadillacs
with wraparound chrome exteriors of nineteen-thirty-one
to banquets on high holidays
eating turkey   chicken   goose with mushrooms
"a fish soup on which floated lakes of lemon juice"
drank velvety madeira booze from Canada cigars of J. P.
      Morgan sniffed cocaine sucked oranges
or dropped peels into their vodka
would wear a deluxe striped suit made of english navy
but with a head for business
Jews moved past el trains blasting tommy guns

other Jews made movies
ran after black girls   did a buck & wing
for Roman gangsters
toasted their mothers with hunky wines
that smelled of sun & bedbugs
of which the father of the dead man wrote in journal
"my child brings solace to a heavy heart
"his intense physicality
"not Jewish truly but tendering a dream of
"strength   resilience   broken promises
"a horsecock strapped between his legs
"in tribute   & my secret joy too
"seeing his dead frame surrounded
"by a thousand blossoms roses of old Poland
"a choir like the Warsaw Synagogue
"led by Sirota   bursts into songs of angels
"flashbulbs from fifty cameras pop
"blinding the humble button operators workers
"in black jackets & silk lapels some
"with yellow shoes   milk-stained wives   outclassed
"outdistanced by that stud in coffin
"whose hair pasted back still smells of
"whorehouse evenings along Atlantic Avenue
"not Moldavanka mad Odessa nights
"remembered the enforcers lift his coffin
"sweat stains the armpits of orange-colored suits
"strawberry vests   blue leather shoes
"& under the shirtcuff of the murdered son
"a diamond-studded bracelet"   thus
Babel or an uncle
might have written though the flesh
retreats from these as other
killers Jews who frightened the round-cheeked schoolboy
with gangster visions   of concrete
bodies into Catskill lakes

their fathers stood above & threw
lint from old pockets into
praying for joy   deliverance
from America the beautiful
oppressor riding in white convertible
up streets of Brownsville
the eagle of the golden States hooked on his arm
& hungry   diving
on faces that he hates
of Jew & Gentile
first searches their hearts for "freedom"
& the happy buck

PORTRAIT OF A JEW OLD COUNTRY STYLE

visitor to warsaw
                old man with open fly
        flesh girls could suck
                mothers would die to catch sight of
sometimes would pass your door
                his song was
        a generation is a day, time floweth
coldly he blew his nose
reached a hand around his high round waist
        money was pinned to caftan
                aches & pains
a jew's a jew he says
love brings him to the words he needs
                but sadly
        no
                I cannot stay

for breakfast loving
the taste of duck eggs loving
little rolls & butter
loving cereals in metal pans
he tells them
all we touch is love
& feeds us
this is a portrait of a jew old country style
the gentile will fail to understand
the jew come on better days will run from it
how real
the grandfathers become

my grandfather the baker son of bakers
YOSEL DOVID ben SHMIEL
who was a hasid at the court in Rizhyn
came to U.S.A. circa 1913
but found the country godless
tho he worked in leather
shoes were the craft all our friends
got into first
like his brother-in-law we called
THE UNCLE
I remember in a basement shop
somewhere "downtown"
bent over shoes he stitched
how many years would pass
till nineteen-fifty maybe
when I saw him last
his lungs gone in east bronx tenement
he slept behind a curtain
seeing me he thought
I was my brother   old & crazy
he was the oldest jew I knew
my grandfather had died

in nineteen-twenty
on the night my parents
ran to warsaw
to get married   my father
left for U.S.A. the next day
no one told him of his father's death
he would never be a talmudist
would go from shoes
to insurance
from insurance back to shoes
later an entrepreneur & bust
he was always clean
shaven   my grandmother
the religious one I mean
saw the first beard
I'd ever grown   got angry
"jews dont wear beards"
(she said) no
not in golden U.S.A.
the old man had fled from
to his Polish death

for which reason I deny autobiography
or that the life of a man
matters more or less
        "We are all one man"
        Cezanne said
I count the failures of these jews
as proof of their election
they are divine because they all die
                              screaming
            like the first
universal jew
        the gentiles
            will tell you had some special deal

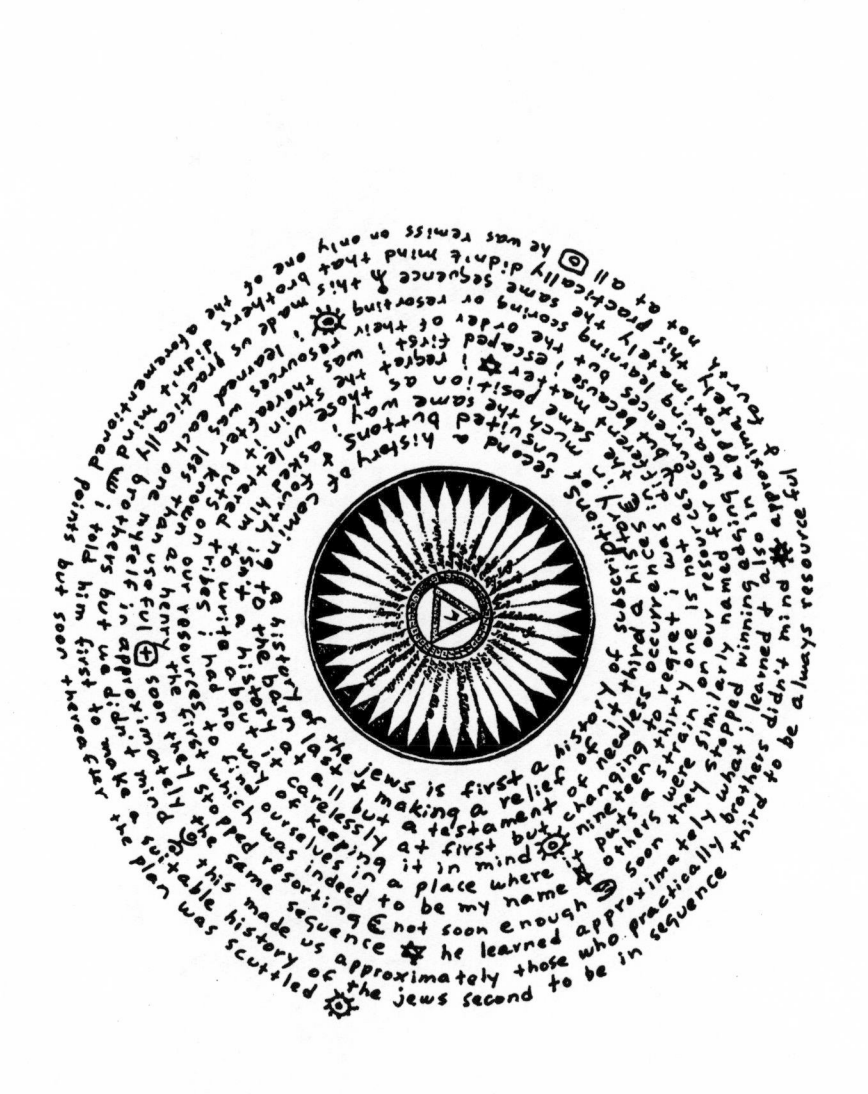

a history of the jews is first a history of subscription ✡ third historic occurrences changing to regret; i was not careful at first but nineteen thirty one puts a strain on our resources soon others were similarly named what they stopped winning adding admitting brothers didn't mind also approximately third to be a always resourceful

a history of the jews is first ✡ making a relief of it ✡ a testament but it all but carelessly at first but ✡ the history it in mind ✡ way of keeping it in a place where ✡ kind of ourselves which was indeed stopped resorting ⊂ not soon enough ✡ to be my name ✡ he learned approximately those who practically ✡ the same sequence this made us history of approximately ✡ the plan was scuttled ✡ the history of the jews second to be in sequence

a history of coming ♥ unsuited butting patiently ♥ i asked him ✡ to write a history but ✡ i had to omit titles ✡ our resources ♥ henry the first ⊕ soon useful but he didn't want to make a suitable but hereafter him first ⊕ Plot points but soon

A BOOK OF HISTORIES

HISTORY ONE

His childhood ambition had been to become a saint.

Hay covered the synagogue floor. It was an old synagogue, the ark carved by an Italian master. On one of the walls hung the matzo eaten at the end of the Passover seder. A metal vase filled with sand contained the prepuces of circumcised infants.

She told him she was Lilith & that if he let her go she would teach him all her names. The names she wrote down were

LILITH	ABITR	ABITO	AMORFO
KKODS	IKPODO	AYYLO	PTROTA
ABNUKTA	STRINA	KALI	PTUZA
	TLTOI-PRITSA.		

He told her he was Elijah.

. . . drinking beer & munching nuts

He had also warned me to be sure that the boiled milk had formed a skin.

long hose
½ shoes
sash about the loins
skullcap beneath a velvet hat
kerchief around neck
metal-rimmed spectacles

He loved to play chess & to make up riddles. "Three entered a cave & five came out"—the answer was Lot & his daughters. Or "what is that which is produced from the ground, yet man produces it, while its food is the fruit of the ground?" "A wick." Or "who was he that was born & died not?" Answer: Elijah & the Messiah.

someone had told me that if I were to light 40 candles & recite a secret incantation he would die

HISTORY TWO

The binding prevented the child from putting its toes into its mouth; also from touching its face with its fingers which may just before have touched its crotch or its toes.

old-fashioned gaberdine
a velvet hat with a high crown
½ boots, pantaloons & white socks

His ritual fringes reached below his knees.

The body was washed in warm water, scented with spices, & then a beaten egg was used as an additional cleansing agent.

Then one of the beadles would remove his boots & walk over the tablecloth in stocking feet, pouring wine for everyone.

Ordinarily she was a quiet girl, but suddenly she would begin to howl like a dog & to speak with a man's voice. Then she sang like a cantor, & her voice was as powerful as the roar of a lion.

"Arise, Rabbi Chisqiah, & stand in thy place & declare the worthiness of this part of the holy beard."

Rabbi Chisqiah arose, & began his speech & said, "I am my beloved's, & his desire is toward me."

. . . by their very exterior you could tell that these were no lovers of water & to your distress you often knew it with your eyes closed

how in Galicia, before a child was suckled, they placed part of a honeycomb in its cradle

The men of the congregation, having a quite different conception of the meaning of this anniversary, arrived with their pockets stuffed with thistles, which they proceeded to toss into each other's beards. When they ran out of thistles, they ripped the plaster from the walls & threw it

He had found an ancient commentary which declared that when Javan would be at war with Ishmael, the deliverance would come. And now he had heard, during a conversation in the ritual baths, that Russia & Turkey were on the point of war. Russia was of course Javan, & it had always been known that Turkey was descended from Ishmael, the son of Hagar, the handmaid of Sarah.

"It cannot be otherwise," the Rabbi muttered, & his excitement increased.

hernia
hemorrhoids

He took the torah scroll & hurled it to the ground, & then he had to fast for 40 days as a penance.

HISTORY THREE

They covered the mirrors with towels, drew the blinds, knocked over the chairs, broke the dishes, & stopped the clock. Then he put on a pair of felt slippers, to accompany the coffin.

"I eat only once a day, at four o'clock. For four years now."

. . . he burst into laughter finding that he had jewish hair, jewish eyes, a long Jewish nose

an enema of lukewarm water & camomile, & sometimes added garlic

He drove off at top speed to New Court, where he arrived just before four o'clock in the afternoon. One of the porters immediately announced him to the head of the firm, whom he told that the Prime Minister wanted £4,000,000 the next day, & why. Baron Lionel picked up a muscatel grape, ate it, threw out the skin, & said, deliberately:

"What is your security?"

"The British Government," replied Corry.

Cutters
Jacket Pressers
Underpressers
Skirt Pressers
Skirt Basters
Skirt Finishers
Buttonhole Makers

While in one corner some stood at prayers, in other corners Jews ate
& drank, drove bargains, argued & bought hot, peppered peas from
an old woman who kept a supply under a mass of rags.

another tradition runneth thus: whiteness in whiteness & whiteness
which includeth all other whiteness

There had been few Jews where he came from. In the course of the
centuries their outward appearance had become Europeanized & had
taken on a human look, so you might even have taken them for
Germans. Then later, strolling through Vienna's inner city, he had
suddenly encountered an apparition in a black caftan & black hair-
locks. Was this a Jew? he thought. They hadn't looked that way in
Linz. He observed the man furtively & cautiously, but the longer he
stared, the more his first question assumed a new form: Was this a
German?

. . . an awning of white silk or satin, supported on four poles & embroidered with the words, THE VOICE OF MIRTH & THE VOICE OF JOY, THE VOICE OF THE BRIDEGROOM & THE VOICE OF THE BRIDE; also with flowers & green leaves . . .

Rabbi Shimeon began, & said: Woe unto him who extendeth his hand unto that most glorious supernal beard of the Holy Ancient One, the concealed of all.

      This is the praise of that beard; the beard which is concealed & most precious in all its dispositions; the beard which neither the superiors have known; the beard which is the praise of all praise; the beard to which neither man, nor prophet, nor saint hath approached as to behold it.

      The beard, whose long hairs hang down even unto the breast, white as snow; the adornment of adornments, the concealment of concealments, the truth of all truths.

. . . he was like a man who takes a ritual bath while holding an unclean reptile in his hand . . .

rice boiled in milk

HISTORY FOUR

There was the rabbi, for example, who said you mustn't urinate in the snow on the Sabbath because it resembles plowing . . .

Once, he told me, while studying the law in the Valley of Genusan, he saw a man climbing a tree. The man found a bird's nest in the tree, & taking the mother with the young ones, he still departed in peace. He saw another man who finding a bird's nest followed the Bible's command & took the young only, allowing the mother to fly away— & yet a serpent stung him as he descended & he died. "Now," he said, "where is the Bible's truth & promises? Is it not written, 'And the young thou mayest take to thyself, but the mother thou shalt surely let go, that it may be well with thee & thou mayest live many days.' Now, where is the long life to this man who followed the precept, while the one who transgressed it is unhurt?"

Their fur coats, old, & fur hats, older, made a pile on a chair. Nails on the wall were the hangers, but chairs were better. Around the talkers in the café were bits of lemon, crumbs of cake, wetted lumps of sugar.

The doctor said: "I was told many times about women who wake their husbands up in the middle of the night—& then all she needs to come is for her husband to move near her."

two quadrangular diapers, one warm one of flannel, the other of linen, & a quadrangular piece of waterproof oilcloth. also a pillow stuffed with feathers

When her oldest son was 2½ years old, they went to the park for a walk. She led him, holding his hand. Whenever the child saw a small or large puddle he encircled it very carefully, in order not to soil his shoes. She always paid a lot of attention to the cleanliness of her boys.

In the women's rooms, where the bride was being prepared for the ceremony, it was cool & spacious. Girls danced together, lifting up the ends of their ballooning skirts; or else they stopped & talked affectedly with the musicians, trying to make their Yiddish sound like German.

awkward in her emotion she had slipped her face under the man's beard & left it buried there . . . her hands were clasped at the small of his back. As he dared a timid caress, barely sensual, on Judith's white neck, a question crossed his mind: Does God, blessed be his name, wish the death of infants?

With a sudden gesture, partly of shyness, partly the result of long training, he covered his eyes in order not to look at a woman, stepped aside, & murmured: "Good evening."

. . . the gutters, where dead horses lay for days or until a special truck came along to haul them off . . .

They conducted the queen to Solomon, who had gone to sit in a house of glass, to receive her. The queen was deceived by an illusion. She thought the king was sitting in water, & as she stepped across to him she raised her garment to keep it dry. On her bared feet the king noticed hair, & said to her: "Thy beauty is the beauty of a woman, but thy hair is masculine; hair is an ornament to a man, but it disfigures a woman."

And the sages said: "Make for me an opening as wide as the eye of a needle, & I shall make an opening for you as wide as the door of a chamber."

. . . later he was also nicknamed the Dancer of God

HISTORY FIVE

He wore a hat in the rabbinic style, but his alpaca jacket reached only to his knees, in the German fashion.

His trousers were striped, his boots glistened.

But he also had white earlocks.

Very frequently he would purify himself in the ritual bath: he would learn by heart & repeat the fantastic names of angels: & he would often deprive himself of meals.

When he was a child he had pictured God as living in the moon. You know—he said—the face in the moon. There was a saying that God looks down from the moon, & he had pictured him that way.

The hut in which he lived was ice-cold. The windows were stopped up with cushions, & the smoke of the kitchen had blackened the walls. Wild mushrooms & toadstools sprouted on the dank, earthen floor. His second wife, a lean, haggard woman, sat on a low chair, pushing her hanging breast against a baby's mouth, & crying:
        "Suck, draw, draw the life out of me!"

whenever he saw his own excreta he threw up

Moreover he spied a skull floating on the face of the water, he said to it: "For drowning others you were drowned; & in the end those who drowned you will be drowned."

The tsaddik shut himself up in his room, & it was said that the floor was covered with dust & never swept. Large mice used to run around,

& old ugly grey frogs jumped in dark corners. The lonesome tsaddik treated them like well-groomed dogs. His disciples said that the frogs & mice were the souls of sinful, deceased hasidim.

Among them was one young beggar, supposedly released from an insane asylum, with a very beautiful & strong tenor voice. Whenever someone refused him charity he would intone the prayer for the dead at the top of his lungs. People stricken with awe gave him what he wanted & ran away.

"When I was born," he told George Cornwallis-West late in life, "I was so beautiful that my co-religionists took me for the Messiah. But they wouldn't think so now, would they?" he added ruefully.

Sleeping that night on the floor of a damp country synagogue, he had been awakened suddenly by a sound of distant singing. He followed it across the room to the great wooden ark of the covenant, whose doors swung open as he reached them. Inside he saw a blue light dancing before the scrolls of the law, & a woman's voice sang loudly: "I Am Afire with Love." It was the most beautiful thing he had ever seen.

not a mere fortuitous aggregation of individuals but a sacred society—a self-dedicated "kingdom of priests"

HISTORY SIX

She would drive off to the Odessa quarries, sit drinking tea with Jews at the Bear Café, buy smuggled goods on the waterfront . . .

But the serious cafés were usually up one flight—on Division Street, Allen Street, Orchard Street, Canal Street, or on Chatham Square.

he was wearing a brown jacket, cream-colored pants, & raspberry-red shoes

Machines, needles, thread, pressing cloth, oil, sponges . . . often the workers brought their own machines, as well as the needles & thread.

When they saw her in the distance, mothers would exclaim, "The demon!" & would pull their children into the house. Under their breath they muttered: "Salt in your eyes! Pepper in your nose!"

also cafés for domino players who drank nothing alcoholic & seldom talked

Two chinamen in bowler hats, holding loaves of bread under their arms, stood on the corner of Sadoraga Street. With their frosty nails, they marked off slivers of the loaf to lure the passing Jewish prostitutes. The women passed by them in a silent procession.

There was the Odessa Café on East Broadway. . . . Others were called Krakow, Moscow, Kiev, Lublin, & Warsaw. . . .

He brought two seamen along with him—an Englishman & a Malay—& the three of them dragged a case of contraband goods from Port Said into the yard. The case was heavy & they dropped it & out tumbled some cigars entangled in Japanese silk.

. . . the Rutgers Street Public Bath

He borrowed a comb & a necktie from an obliging detective, dusted off his shoes & faced the press, his usual, debonair self.

. . . bohemian cafés . . . noisy with dancers & accordionists

His ideals of life resolved themselves into money to spend, beautiful women to enjoy, silk underclothes, & places to go in style.

After dinner he settled in an armchair & opened a thin volume. His gangster friend had recommended *The Prince* as a way of gaining insight into the Italian mind.

"& Joseph will get a first-class funeral—there'll be six horses like six lions, & two carriages for the wreaths, & the choir from the Brodsky synagogue, & Minkovsky in person will sing over your late son."

green horn
maki
griner
griner tukes

—How old were you when your mother stopped punishing you?

—When I was old enough to defend myself—then she stopped. I must have been about 16.

—Did she ever spank you?

—She *beat* me, & she threw things at me, & she hit me with sticks, & she punched me, & she pulled my hair.

With an ancient Spanish dagger—none from Sicily was available— Trafficante cut his left wrist, allowed the blood to flow, & wet his right hand in the crimson stream. Then he held up the bloody hand.

"So long as the blood flows in my body," he intoned solemnly, "do I, Santo Trafficante, swear allegiance to the will of Meyer Lansky & the organization he represents. If I violate this oath, may I burn in hell forever."

Tourine witnessed the signature with an X in ink. Sam Tucker produced a band-aid, & the two Mafia leaders hurried out.

. . . a play called *Demented America*—his final play

HISTORY SEVEN

". . . During the second week the power became so strong in me that I couldn't manage to write down all the combinations of letters wch automatically spurted out of my pen. . . . When I came to the night in wch this power was conferred on me, & Midnight had passed, I set out to take up the Great Name of God, consisting of 72 Names, permuting & combining it. But when I had done this for a little while, the letters took on the shape of great mountains, strong trembling seized me & I could summon no strength, my hair stood on end, & it was as if I were not in this world. Then something resembling speech came to my lips & I forced them to move. I said: 'This is indeed the spirit of wisdom.' "

a head of a carp wrapped in cabbage leaves

Sometimes it happened that during the merchant's travels in the forests a young peasant woman would wait on him, the wife of some innkeeper: she would smile up at him as she drew the long boots off his feet before he went to bed: she would beg him to raise her husband's pay. Then he did not say no: nor did he refuse to let her kiss his hand out of gratitude when he had put out the light.

. . . picking cucumbers out of a barrel of brine

If anyone came within ten feet of him during prayer or before it, the rabbi would shout words like "cattle" or "robbers" & would sometimes slip off his belt & strike whoever was in his way.

. . . in the evening i brought her a white loaf as well as a dark one . . . also poppy seed rolls i baked myself . . . i thieved because of her & swiped everything i could lay my hands on . . . macaroons . . . raisins . . . almonds . . . cakes . . . i hope i may be forgiven for stealing from the saturday pots the women left to warm in the baker's oven . . . i would take out scraps of meat . . . a chunk of pudding . . . a chicken leg or head . . . a piece of tripe . . . whatever I could nip quickly . . . she ate & became fat & handsome . . .

Not only the gateway, the entire courtyard was filled with obstacles. Servant girls sang, & Reb Moishe stopped his ears, for the voice of woman leads to lewdness. The sound of gramophones came thru open windows, & sometimes a troop of magicians & acrobats gave a performance in the courtyard; a half-naked girl, wearing short breeches & a beaded jacket walked on her hands. Every step of the way was fraught with danger. Servants sat on the stairs, grating horse-radish & slicing onions. All the world's females seemed to be waylaying Reb Moishe, trying to deflect him from the narrow path of righteousness & lead him to Gehenna. But Reb Moishe carried his weapon—his walking stick. He closed his eyes & pounded the stone flags with his stick.

vodka & currant cake

Zanvl took hold of the bag; then with the swiftness of a young gypsy he lifted the door off the hinges. Warm steam beat into his face. He took out the whiskey, made the horses drunk, & put shoes on their feet. Then he led them softly out of the stable.

We used to make holes in the sand with the heels of our boots. All the holes had to be approximately the same size. Then we would all piss into these holes. The one who filled his hole first was the winner.

Every morning he went from door to door after he had prepared the synagogue. He tapped on the shutters with his wooden hammer & called out weakly: "Jews, rise! It is time to serve God."

a silken man

he had completely incarnated himself into a sacred lemon

COKBOY

COKBOY   Part One

saddlesore I came
a jew among
the indians
vot em I doink in dis strange place
mit deez pipple mit strange eyes
could be it's trouble
could be   could be
(he says) a shadow
ariseth from his buckwheat
has tomahawk in hand
shadow of an axe inside his right eye
of a fountain pen inside his left
vot em I doink here
how vass I lost tzu get here
am a hundred men
a hundred fifty different shadows
jews & gentiles
who bring the Law to Wilderness
(he says) this man
is me   my grandfather
& other men-of-letters
men with letters carrying the mail
lithuanian pony-express riders
the financially crazed Buffalo Bill
still riding in the lead
hours before avenging the death of Custer

making the first 3-D movie of those wars
or years before it
the numbers vanishing in kabbalistic time
that brings all men together
& the lonely rider
saddlesore
is me   my grandfather
& other men-of-letters
jews & gentiles entering
the domain of Indian
who bring the Law to Wilderness
in gold mines & shaky stores
the fur trade heavy agriculture
ballots bullets barbers
who threaten my beard your hair
but patronize me
& will make our kind the Senator from Arizona
the champion of their Law
who hates us both
but dresses as a jew one day an indian
the next a little christian shmuck
vot em I doink here
dis place is maybe crazy
has all the letters going backwards
(he says) so who can read the signboards
to the desert
who can shake his way out of the woods
ford streams the grandmothers
were living near
with snakes inside their cunts
teeth maybe
maybe chainsaws
when the Baal Shem visited America

he wore a shtreiml
the locals all thought he was a cowboy
maybe from Mexico
"a cokboy?"
no a cowboy
I will be more than a credit to my community
& race
but will search for my brother Esau among these redmen
their nocturnal fires I will share
piss strained from my holy cock
will bear seed of Adonoi
& feed them visions
I will fill full a clamshell
will pass it around from mouth to mouth
we will watch the moonrise
through each other's eyes
the distances vanishing in kabbalistic time
(he says) the old man watches
from the cliffs a city
overcome with light
the man & the city disappear
be looks & sees another city
this one is made of glass
inside the buildings stand
immobile statues
brown-skinned faces
catch the light
an elevator
moving up & down
in the vision of the Cuna *nele*
the vision of my grandfather
vision of the Baal Shem in America
the slaves in steerage

what have they seen in common
by what light their eyes
have opened into stars
I wouldn't know
what I was doing here
this place has all the letters going
backwards a reverse in time
towards wilderness
the old jew strains at his gaberdine
it parts for him
his spirit rushes up the mountainside
& meets an eagle
no an iggle
captains   commanders   dollinks   delicious madmen
murderers opening the continent up to exploitation
cease & desist (he says)
let's speak (he says)
feels like a little gas down here (he says)
(can't face the mirror without crying)
& the iggle lifts him
like an elevator
to a safe place above the sunrise
there gives a song to him
the Baal Shem's song
repeated without words for centuries
"hey heya heya" but translates it
as "yuh-buh-buh-buh-buh-buh-bum"
when the Baal Shem (yuh-buh) learns to do a bundle
what does the Baal Shem (buh-buh) put into the bundle?
silk of his prayershawl-bag beneath
cover of beaverskin above
savor of esrog fruit within
horn of a mountaingoat between

feather of dove around the sides
clove of a Polish garlic at its heart
he wears when traveling
in journeys through kabbalistic forests
cavalry of the Tsars on every side
men with fat moustaches yellow eyes & sabers
who stalk the gentle soul
at night through the Wyoming steppes
(he says) vot em I doink here
I could not find mine het
would search the countryside on hands & knees
until   behind a rock in Cody
old indian steps forth
the prophecies of both join at this point
like smoke a pipe is held
between them dribbles through their lips
the keen tobacco
"cowboy?"
cokboy (says the Baal Shem)
places a walnut in his handkerchief & cracks it
on a boulder each one eats
the indian draws forth a deck of cards
& shuffles
"game?"
they play at wolves & lambs
the fire crackles in the pripitchok
in a large tent somewhere in America
the story of the coming-forth begins

COKBOY   PART TWO

comes a brown
wind curling from
tense tissues sphincter
opened over the whole continental
divide & shot the people up
plop plop a little girl emergeth
she with the beaver tits nose furry
eyes of the Redman's
Sabbath
gropes down the corridor
(sez) hallo doctor
got a hand to spare?
doctor sez hokay
—yas doctor
hand up her bush
he pulls
a baby   howling
in lamplight a little Moses
now the Cacique's daughter laugheth
—oh doctor not so-o hard
so hard America is born
so hard the Baal Shem dreams about it
200 years later
in Vitebsk
(he was in correspondence with Wm Blake
appeared on Peckham Rye
—yes fully clothed! —
& was his angel)
angel says his mother
smiling proud

she sees his little foot
break through
her crotch an itching
races up her ribs
America is born
the Baal Shem is a beaver
(happened while the Indian talked
chanted behind Cody
the mad jew slid to life
past pink styrofoam snow of her body's
channels
the freaky passageways
unlit unloved
like gums of an old woman
teeth were ripped from
ages gone) into
another kind of world
he hurtles
does reawaken in the female swamp
a beaver amongst the rushes
—momma!—calls the Baal Shem
—mommeleh!
vot em I doink here
I hev become mine beard
(he says) the blind world shines on him
water runs through his mouth
down belly it is dark
a darkness (fur is dark
& hides the skin & blood
a universal fur
but leaves one hole
to open from the body's
darkness pushing

into light)

erupts

like great cock of the primal beings

red & smooth like copper

of the sun's red eye at night

old Beaver lugs it in his hand

I am myself   my grandfather

(he sings) my name is Cokboy

—COKBOY, understand?

I leave my grandmother in the female swamp

will be the Great Deliverer someday yuh-buh-bum

even might find a jar of honey might stick my prick in my prick might
    tingle might it not tickle me the bees find out about it & sting the
    knob it grows a second a dozen or so knobs along its length are
    maybe 30 knobs

so what's the use I ask maybe will try again I drag it red & sore behind
    me so vulnerable I have become in this hot climate shitting &
    farting shooting marbles was opening my mouth & coming in it

the blackbird shits o not so fast love into my hat my eyes turn white
    wood-lilies are growing from them a slavic birth I can't deny so
    tender in my eyes tender the native turds come floating

& across America in an outrage uselessly I shout against the Sun you
    are no longer my father Moon you are no longer my mother I
    have left you have gone out jaunty with cock slung over shoulder
    this is the journey your young men will take

(says Beaver) makes it to the hut where that old woman lives apron
    over her belly carp in oven maybe fried bread fat fat little moth-
    er don't mind if I drop a stone onto your brains your daughters
    be back later little hot girls I ride on pretending I was you I suck
    their ears & scream o put me lower down love o my cock inside

& have to cool it

I cool it

in waters where a princess

daughter of a chief
went bathing
lethal & innocent the cock
has found its mark
(his train has reached Topeka
Custer is dead)
& enters the bridegroom's quarters
darkness her flesh prepared for it
by new moon
in her abdomen a sliver
grows
a silver dollar over Barstow
lighting the Marriage of America
in kabbalistic time
(says Cokboy) you are the daughter of
the mountain
now will I take thee to my father's tribe
to do the snake dance
o jewish feet of El go crazy
in his mind
o
El
o
Him
I carry in my knapsack
dirty pictures land grants
(but further back her people
gun for him
how should they feel
seeing their daughter in arms of
Cokboy
—C-O-C-K, understand?—)
thou art become my Father's bride
are wedded to (ugh) Christian god

forever
bye bye I got to run now
engagements await us in Salt Lake City
industry riseth everywhere
arrows strike concrete
never shall bruise my sweetie's flesh
(says Cokboy) on horse
up river he makes his way
past mining camps Polacks were panning gold in
& other pure products of America
o prospectors o Anglo Saxons
baby-faced dumplings who pacified the west
with gattling guns with bounties for hides of babes
mothers' vulvas made baseballs to their lust
o bringers of civilization heros heros
I will fight my way past you who guard the sacred border
last frontier village of my dreams
with shootouts tyrannies
(he cries) who had escaped the law
or brought it with him
how vass I lost tzu get here
was luckless
on a mountain & kept from
true entry to the west true paradise
like Moses in the Rockies who stares at California spooky in
          the jewish light
of horns atop my head great orange freeways of the mind
America disaster
America disaster
America disaster
America disaster
where he can watch the sun go down
in desert

Cokboy asleep (they ask)
awake (cries Cokboy)
only his beard has left him
like his own   his grandfather's
ghost of Ishi was waiting on the crest
looked like a Jew
but silent
was silent in America
guess I got nothing left to say

KHURBN

Since the hidden is bottomless, totality is more
invisible than visible.

—CLAYTON ESHLEMAN

IN 1987 I WAS A DECADE, more, past *Poland/1931*. I went to Poland for the first time & to the small town, Ostrow-Mazowiecka, sixty miles northeast of Warsaw, from which my parents had come in 1920. The town was there and the street, Miodowa (meaning "honey"), where my father's parents had a bakery. I hadn't realized that the town was only fifteen miles from Treblinka, but when we went there (as we had to), there was only an empty field & the thousands of large stones that make up the memorial. We were the only ones there except for a group of three people—another family perhaps—who seemed to be picnicking at the side. This was in sharp contrast to the crowds of tourists at Auschwitz (Oswiecim) & to the fullness of the other Poland I had once imagined. The absence of the living seemed to create a vacuum in which the dead—the dibbiks who had died before their time—were free to speak. It wasn't the first time that I thought of poetry as the language of the dead, but never so powerfully as now. Those in my own family had died without a trace—with one exception: an uncle who had gone to the woods with a group of Jewish partisans and who, when he heard that his wife and children were mur-dered at Treblinka, drank himself blind in a deserted cellar & blew his brains out. That, anyway, was how the story had come back to us, a long time before I had ever heard a word like holocaust. It was a word with which I never felt comfortable: too Christian & too beautiful, too much smacking of a "sacrifice" I didn't & still don't understand. The word with which we spoke of it was the Yiddish-Hebrew word, *khurbn* (khurban), & it was this word that was with me all the time we stayed in Poland. When I was writing *Poland/1931*, at a great distance from the place, I decided deliberately that that was not to be a poem about the "holocaust." There was a reason for that, I think, as there is now for allowing my uncle's khurbn to speak through me. The poems that I first began to hear at Treblinka are the clearest message I have ever gotten about why I write poetry. They are an answer also to the proposition—by Adorno & others—that poetry cannot or should not be written after Auschwitz. Our search since then has been for the origins of poetry, not only as a willful desire to wipe the slate clean but as a recognition of those other voices & the scraps of poems they left behind them in the mud.

IN THE DARK WORD, KHURBN
all their lights went out

their words were silences,
memories
drifting along the horse roads
onto malkiner street

a disaster in the mother's tongue
her words emptied
by speaking

returning to a single word
the child word
spoken, redeyed on
the frozen pond

was how they spoke it,
how I would take it from your voice
& cradle it

that ancient & dark word

those who spoke it in the old days
now held their tongues

DOS OYSLEYDIKN (THE EMPTYING)

at honey street in ostrova
where did the honey people go?
empty   empty
miodowa empty
empty bakery & empty road to warsaw
yellow wooden houses & houses plastered up with stucco
the shadow of an empty name still on their doors
shadai & shadow shattering the mother tongue
the mother's tongue but empty
the way the streets are empty where we walk
pushing past crowds of children
old women airing themselves outside the city hall
old farmers riding empty carts down empty roads
who don't dispel but make an emptiness
a taste of empty honey
empty rolls you push your fingers through
empty sorrel soup dribbling from their empty mouths
defining some other poland
lost to us the way the moon
is lost to us
the empty clock tower measuring her light four ways
sorrel in gardens mother of god at roadsides
in the reflection of the empty trains
only the cattle bellow in
like jews the dew-eyed wanderers
still present   still the flies
cover their eyeballs
the trains drive eastward, falling
down a hole (a holocaust) of empty houses
of empty ladders leaning against haystacks no one climbs

empty ostrova & empty ostrolenka
old houses empty in the woods near vyzhkov
dachas the peasants would rent to you
& sleep in stables
the bialo forest spreading to every side
retreating the closer we come to it to claim it
empty oaks & empty fir trees
a man in an empty ditch who reads a book
the way the jews once read
in the cold polish light   the fathers sat there too
the mothers posed at the woods' edge
the road led brightly to treblinka
& other towns   beaches at brok
along the bug
marshes with cattails
cows tied to trees
past which their ghosts walk
their ghosts refuse to walk
tomorrow in empty fields of poland
still cold against their feet
an empty pump black water drips from
will form a hill of ice
the porters will dissolve with burning sticks
they will find a babe's face at the bottom
invisible & frozen imprinted in the rock

... PASSING CHELMNO ON THE MAIN ROAD DRIVING PAST IT ...

In May,
along the road to Warsaw,

little ghosts
of Lidice.

A row of peasants
cutting up the earth

on bended
knees.

A man spiffs up
a roadside shrine,

leaving a bunch of
tacky flowers.

Little figures
bathing in the Warta.

Little thought
to what was there.

HIDDEN IN WOODS   BAGGED
like an Indian

a cry (darkest in
the pauses)

cannot be heard   But inward
he discerns it

what his life had been
& several   trusting in him

(children

or the dead) life's burden
I cannot escape it any longer

in a vodka sleep (the cry
cutting still deeper

into his bones)   Bright spots
a zohar of possibilities

a father's cry

(oh mother hold me) how I have lost
my tongue

my hand chewed down
to the bone   must bellow

like a heifer
& crawling through their blood

my children severed from me
(their souls

stuck in my mouth   teeth
frozen

the room turns to ice

in moonlight

it flies through the woods

a cry   a spirit
his death turns loose

with no roots
runs deeper   the cry you can hear

is no cry

DOS GESHRAY (THE SCREAM)

Erd, zolst nit tsudekn mayn blut
un zol nit kayn ort zayn far mayn geshray
(Job 16:18)

"practice your scream" I said
(why did I say it?)
because it was his scream & wasn't my own
it hovered between us   bright
to our senses always bright it held
the center place
then somebody else came up & stared
deep in his eyes there found a memory
of horses galloping faster the wheels dyed red
behind them   the poles had reserved
a feast day but the jew
locked in his closet screamed
into his vest a scream
that had no sound therefore
spiraled around the world
so wild that it shattered stones
it made the shoes piled in the doorway
scatter their nails   things testify
—the law declares it—
shoes & those dearer objects
like hair & teeth do
by their presence
I cannot say that they share the pain
or show it not even the photos
in which the expressions of the dead shine forth
the crutches by their mass the prosthetic limbs by theirs

bear witness the eyeglasses bear witness
the suitcases the children's shoes the german tourists
in the stage set oshvientsim had become
the letters over its gates still glowing
still writ large
ARBEIT MACHT FREI
& to the side   HOTEL
and GASTRONOMIC BAR
the spirit of the place dissolving
indifferent to his presence
there with the other ghosts
the uncle   grieving
his eyelids turning brown an eye
protruding from his rump
this man whose body
is a crab's
his gut turned outward
the pink flesh of his children
hanging from him
that his knees slide up against
there is no holocaust
for these   but khurbn only
the word still spoken by the dead
who say   my khurbn
& my children's khurbn
it is the only word that the poem allows
because it is their own
the word as prelude to the scream
it enters
through the asshole
circles along the gut
into the throat
& breaks out

in a cry   a scream
it is his scream that shakes me
weeping in   oshvientsim
& that allows the poem to come

DIBBUKIM (DIBBIKS)

spirits of the dead   lights
flickering (he said) their ruakh
will never leave the earth
instead they crowd the forests the fields
around the privies the hapless spirits
wait millions of souls
turned into ghosts at once
the air is full of them
they are standing each one beside a tree
under its shadows or the moon's
but they cast no shadows of their own
this moment & the next they are pretending
to be rocks   but who is fooled
who is fooled here   by the dead   the jews
the gypsies   the leadeyed polish patriot
living beings reduced to symbols
of what it had been to be alive
"o do not touch them" the mother cries
fitful, as almost in a dream
she draws the child's hand to her heart
in terror   but the innocent dead
grow furious they break down doors
drop slime onto your tables
they tear their tongues out by the roots
& smear your lamps your children's lips
with blood a hole drilled in the wall
will not deter them
from stolen homes stone architectures
they hate they are the convoys of the dead
the ghostly drivers still searching

the roads to malkin   ghost carts overturned
ghost autos in blue ditches
if only our eyes were wild enough
to see them our hearts to know their terror
the terror of the man who walks alone
their victim whose house whose skin
they crawl in   incubus & succubus
a dibbik leaping from a cow to lodge inside
his throat   clusters of jews
who swarm here mothers without hair
blackbearded fathers
they lap up fire   water   slime
entangle the hairs of brides
or mourn their clothing hovering
over a field of rags   half-rotted shoes
& tablecloths   old thermos bottles   rings
lost tribes in empty synagogues
at night their voices
carrying across the fields
to rot your kasha your barley
stricken beneath their acid rains
no holocaust because no sacrifice
no sacrifice to give the lie
of meaning   & no meaning   after auschwitz
there is only poetry   no hope
no other language left to heal
no language   & no faces
because no faces left   no names
no sudden recognitions on the street
only the dead still swarming   only khurbn
a dead man in a rabbi's clothes
who squats   outside the mortuary house
who guards their privies who is called

master of shit   an old alarm clock
hung around his neck   who holds
a wreath of leaves under his nose
from eden   "to drive out
"the stinking odor of this world"

THE OTHER SECRET IN THE TRAIL OF MONEY

& all true all true the poet's vision
proven in the scraps. Bank notes & zlotys strewn
over the field. Papers buried. Testaments
to death & to the acquisitive nature of the guards
its passage from hand to hand, to make a picnic
in the Jewish State. Imagine.
That he is again in the field leading to the showers & that the field is
strewn with money. Those who are dead have left it, & the living
bend to pick it up. The rhythms of Gold's orchestra drift past him, as
in the woods sometimes the squeals of children & women or the
deeper bellows of the men. He bends to lift a coin or to remove a bag
of chocolates & raisins from a dead girl's coat. Butter. Cheese. White
rolls. Roast chicken. Cognac. Cream. Sardines. "More sugar & tea
than in the whole Warsaw ghetto." The Jewish workers & their
guards feast in the woods. A child is with them—turns her mouth to
you—that by gematria becomes a hole.

DER GILGUL (THE POSSESSED)

1
he picks a coin up
from the ground

it burns his hand
like ashes it is red

& marks him as it marks
the others   hidden

he is hidden in the forest
in a world of nails

his dibbik fills him

2
Each night another one would hang himself. Airless boxcars.
Kaddish. "What will they do with us?" The brown & black spots on
their bellies. So many clothes. The field was littered. Ten thousand
corpses in one place. Arranged in layers. I am moving down the field
from right to left—reversing myself at every step. The ground
approaches. Money. And still his greatest fear was that he would lose
his shoes.

3
earth, growing fat with
the slime of corpses   green & pink

that ooze like treacle, turn
into a kind of tallow

that are black
at evening   that absorb

all light

NOKH AUSHVITS (AFTER AUSCHWITZ)

the poem is ugly & they make it uglier
wherein the power resides
that duncan did—or didn't—understand
when listening that evening to the other poet read
he said   "that was pure ugliness"   & oh it was
it was   & it made my heart skip a beat
because the poem wouldn't allow it   no
not a moment's grace nor beauty to obstruct
whatever the age demanded   or the poem
shit poured on wall & floor
sex shredded   genitals torn loose by dog claws
& the ugliness that you were to suffer
later   that they had suffered
not as dante dreamed it but in the funnel
they ran through & that the others called
the road to heaven   little hills & holes now
& beneath   upon   among them
broken mirrors kettles pans enameled teapots
the braided candlesticks of sabbath
prayershawl scraps & scraps of bodies   bones
his child's   he said   leaping
into the mud the pool of bones
& slime   the frail limbs separating
each time he pulls at one   the mystery of body
not a mystery   bodies naked   then bodies
boned & rotten   how he must flight
his rage for beauty must make a poem
so ugly it can drive out the other voices
like artaud's squawk the poem addressed
to ugliness   must resist

even the artistry of death   a stage set
at treblinka   ticket windows   a large clock
the signs that read: change for bialystok
but the man cries who has seen
the piles of clothing   jews
it is not good it is your own sad meat
that hangs here   poor & bagged   like animals
the blood coagulated into a jell
an armpit through which a ventricle has burst
& left him dangling screaming
a raw prong stuck through his tongue
another through his scrotal sac   he sees
a mouth   a hole   a red hole
the scarlet remnants of the children's flesh
their eyes like frozen baby scallops
so succulent that the blond ukrainian guard
sulking beneath his parasol leaps up
& sucks them inward past his iron teeth
& down his gullet, shitting
globules of fat & shit
that trickle down the pit in which the victim—
the girl without a tongue—stares up
& reads her final heartbreak

THOSE WHO ARE BEAUTIFUL & THOSE WHO ARE NOT
change places   to relive
a death by excrement

victims thrown into the pit & drowning
in their ordure
suffocating in the body's dross

this is extremity

these images of shit, too raw
for feeling,
that drips onto their faces

women squatting on long planks
to shit "like birds
perched on a telegraph wire"

who daub each other

have no language for the horror
left to speak, the stink
has so much caked their throats,

they who would live with shit
& scrape it
from drinking cups

this is extremity   this place

is where desire ends
where the warm flux inside the corpse
changes to stone

THE DOMAIN OF THE TOTAL CLOSES AROUND THEM   for
there is even   totality here   a parody of telos   of completion
in the monstrous mind of the masters   those who give themselves
        authority
over the rest of life   who dole out life & death   proportioned
to their own appetites as artists   they forge a world   a shadow
        image of our own
& are the artists of the new hell   the angels of the possible the vision
passed from them down to the present   of what art can do what
        constructs of the mind
are thinkable   when power assists their hands   in the delusion of
        the absolute
"a universe of death"   where hell's thrust upward toward the surface
        becomes the vital fact
a row of chimneys spewing flames into the night smoke bursting from
        holes & ditches   swirling swaying coiling above their heads
"the sparks & cinders blinded us" (the scroll reads) "through the
        screened fence of the second crematory we could see figures
        with pitchforks moving against the background of flames
"turning the corpses in the pits so densely packed it seemed that death
        had welded them together"
the faces of the uncovered dead twist in the flames that touch them
seem to come back to life   exuding lymph & fat
that oozes from them   eyes exploding   like the belly
of the pregnant woman   bursting open   now expels
its fetus   that goes up in flames

. . . .

2

but at the camp's outer edge new buildings rise a paradise of painted
       doors
a lane of flowers a pond in which a stone frog sits a little wooden
       bench set at the brink with pastoral animals brave shepherds
it is this other camp that haunts him now that haunts *me* this with its
       sculpted images of jews
the faces sharp & bright that show no trace of suffering but eyes
       aflame turn toward their future
& sing bravely the song of work & death that the masters had
       enjoined that gold had written for them
ecstatic jews in wood & always bowing pointing to the jewish state
       that lies within
yours is the world of art writ large art joined to life until the bound-
       aries split apart
the measure struck by gold's orchestra a sound so sweet that even the
       masters swayed to it
so did the jews bring tears to eyes already dark with smoke so would
       the jews bring tears again
whom later in the market place in krakow we would see anew
their noble wooden faces & marbled eyes fulfilling the dream of life
the gold jews & the jews of death exchanging places
they for whom money lies beneath the field   under the barracks
       floor   & buys them time
the corpses melt   the plaza jews trade garbage in the square
the hapless jews slowly fall backwards & are buried in the ditch
the band is in white dinner jackets trimmed in blue with staves on the
       lapels & trousers blue stripes along the seams
the court jews live in private rooms & give their children educations
       waiting
for the night to come again the cabaret to start its doleful music
       where bad art

to bad art's joined the heart grows murky weeps at its own losses but
drones on

. . . . . .

3
THE SONG

"the sound of workers'
"feet   marching
"faces in ice, dark faces

"battalions on their way
"to work   the faithful
"& the brave   (they say)

"this brings us here,
"treblinka-bound, the end
"a breath away & carried

"in the master's voice
"it is the thunder, is the way
"he looks or we look

"bunched in columns, docile
"docile, must obey or die
"(they say) we do not want

"to leave you   destiny
"is anywhere we turn
"it casts an eye on us,

"will find us waiting here
"faces in ice, battalions
"marching   one final day

.   .   .   .   .   .

4

the assignators even here   breathing thru the lungs of the
ill-fated Max Bielas   handsome man who had a harem
of little jewish boys & dressed them to the delight of
all who visited in perfect white blouses & dark blue hosen
over tummies & butts so round & firm he trembled   yawned
sent them to tend the flock of geese a row of pretty boys
dressed up like princes   & had a fabled dream house
built for them   of roughhewn logs   lace curtains   in which
they slept they sang they waited in the afternoons
for uncle Max to come to them   sweet
german daddy bringing little cakes & *schlag* or letters
from the folks out east   they were his dwarfs & he
their gentle snow white swooning when they pressed around him
when he touched a tiny hand or let his thumb slide down
the young back proffered to him   redfaced   eager   to become
        a victim to his victim
the bright pornography of death implicit in each breath
each word the mind imagines   it is desire that compels him
directs the flow the force engulfing him & them
all in the name of love that has delivered many to this place
as hate has   the goods of the intellect reduced
& bounded   by the craving self   protected from the world
where the mind & the body go astray   theirs is no simple wish
for death or order but toward that greater ugliness
debasement breeds   this that de sade foretold   that the young

mind of isidore ducasse
tracked to his own destruction   so sweet it is so sickening
we pull away from it although it holds us (we who were young enough
      were old enough to be its victims)
it makes us gag & scream here where we listen to the other voices
of those who were abandoned those whom desire fondled
until in the aftermath of his own death his cravings spent the other
      killers entered
restored them to the silent world where no love is
where they were returned to light   & dust   cut loose   in flesh's
      color
into the house of pain

. . . . . .

5
the grandfather who would have carried god with him
into the pit   would he have cursed as I will for him?

or for that uncle who died, surely, with a malediction on his tongue
screamed it until the tongue dissolved the bullet achieved its mark bit
      deeper

into a world of fact (alas) the mind that cries cried out
"the god is real he whom the dead bear with them

"who bear witness to the death of metaphor & cry:
"do not forget us! help us! think of us!"

he is a man called yoshka is a name we share that grandfather & I
name that the jews called jesus that they screamed out of the slime

the world is god's then   & its ugliness   follows from his
therefore they love the female form   the boundaries

no one can know or guess but sometimes discern it in
the mother   she like an absent god   stripped into naked-
          ness

along the fivefold stages of her way the windows tight shut around her
brightly painted the fixed hands of the giant clock still stuck at three

their spirits still wandering who will never rest
babes thrown hapless to the flames the eyes & tongues of the
          old men torn out

o god of caves (the stricken fathers cry) if you are light
then there can be no metaphor

DI MAGILAS FUN AUSHVITS (THE SCROLLS OF AUSCHWITZ)

He had vanished & reappeared in a room no bigger than a giant's hand. Asleep in it. His arms & legs were rusted, his eyes swam in his head like mercury. He was twice forgotten. A stranger to his memory of who he was.

When a man moves up & down across the field, the earth moves with him. The condition is described as double thunder—repeated by the ones called souls, the hopeless dead. It is most likely they who move, the rest is an illusion. The stranger in the giant's hand knows who they are.

Dibbik legions perch on trees. The trees die. Then the sun gives birth to basilisks. A basilisk gives birth to what the rock conceals. True life is punctuated. It eats through time & breeds out of the sun. The sexual is its other head worn on its other body. It is your body too & tries to run from you. You brush against it with your hand.

Once the dibbik was a singular occurrence. It is now repeated many million times as the result of so much early death. Into whom do the dead souls enter? Each one contains a dibbik, or some of them contain a world of dibbiks. Hijikata writes: "To make the gestures of the dead, to die again, to make the dead enact their deaths again, this is what I want to feel. The dead are my teachers & live inside me."

A hand is like a hole. I know it & he knows it too. Was he there? No. No more than I was. But the dead have found him & eaten through his skin. He feels them in the morning when he shits: a gnawing pain beneath his heart. The dead who were burnt alive are still the hapless dead. Thus the ceremony-of-burning is a lie. And thus the holocaust.

In the dream 3000 naked women cry in pain. It is impossible to count them but he does. Their bodies will be used for kindling, their blood for fuel. No one will cry or turn away, but sometimes the wind will force a tear out of his eye, & his tongue & teeth will follow, flying from his mouth. "Ah," the young girl will say, her legs twisted behind her back. "The tear of a live Jew will go with me to my death."

The room he looked into now was still smaller. It looked like a regular shower room with all the accoutrements of a public bathhouse. The walls of the room were covered with small, white tiles. It was very fine, clean work. The floors were covered with orange terra cotta tiles. Nickel-plated metal faucets were set into the ceiling.

It was in Poland that I realized I was haunted. Yes. "A dibbik is in me. A dibbik is in me." It is the condition of our lives for forty years now. Hijikata confirms it for us, that poetry is the speech of ghosts. The shamans in your books confirm it. In *my* books I meant to say. And didn't.

[Gradowski's Testament] A black & white world, sky & earth. The court of angry shadows. These. Broken into. The open mouth of earth prepared to swallow us alive. The last. His world a tinted film. A bent black mass. Black shadows. Swallowed up in railroad cars. Gradowski's testament. Along the white road. Thousands crawling on all fours. Two women at the roadside, crying. People shrunk to half their size. A finger moves across her throat. "Take interest in this document. Keep looking. You will find still more."

From now on we will bury everything in the earth.

DER VIDERSHTAND (THE RESISTANCE)

began with this in olson's words it was
the pre/face   so much fat for soap
superphosphate for soil   fillings & shoes for sale
such fragmentation delivered by whatever means
the scrolls of auschwitz buried   now brought to light
again   the words of zalman lowenthal of poland
who had been dragged into the woods who saw
"the damned plays of liquidation"—incredible (he wrote)
the ocean seeping across the empty field
inside his head   how like a sump   how grungy
the world reduced to yellow flesh & mud
the man in black whose hands are in black gloves
has killed them   the red one
still standing at the gates of warsaw
waits   & the other   at the gates of paris   holds
the dark rule now past the 8th month 1944
a game of shootings hangings gassings burnings
written down   between the wails of the black building
from the time he searched for reasons
for his suffering & wrote
about himself "what happened to that jew?"
or the blond girl now a dibbik asked the question
"mister jew what will they do with us?"
& someone—was it him?—said "garbage"
the resistance beginning with the writing down
that the time & mud have faded
the moon adrift in elul   shining
on a certain man concerned
with history who took the trouble
to assemble pictures   facts   reports

to shield them with his body
"this house" wrote olson "where his life is
"where he dwells against the enemy   the beast"
but sees it crumble sees *them* crumble
all around him   this sparagmos
where the flesh turned yellow from the gas
the fire burst it & the fetus
erupted through the mother's skin
a babe's head that the hair is torn from
& brunner the s.s. survivor used the same word "garbage"
in 1987   thus was the epic verified
& brought into our time   the poem
began with it & followed the movement
of the dead man's hand   as if each written word
had such a hand behind it
that brought the letters & the pain together
written with his blood (the scroll says) in the light
of human bodies burning   but what is interesting
here (he writes) is the psychology of man
who refuses to accept
evil thoughts   no matter how clearly he sees
he speaks   for this is not
the whole truth   the truth as it really exists
is immeasurably more tragic & terrible.   In the notebook
        dig to search
it is by chance that this
is buried   by chance that it comes to light
the poetry is there too
it is in the scraps of language
by which the century is read to us the streets the dogs
the faces fading out the eyes receding
they are the dead & want so much to speak
that all the writing in the world will not contain them

but the dead voice crying in the money field
declares it   makes its resistance still
he says   I want to tell you
what my name is   my name is buried
in the ashes   my name
is not a name

WHAT MAKES HIM KNEEL DOWN IN THE MUD
kneel down in the money field, to lift up
this wet shining coin

as later he would draw
chocolates & raisins from the young girl's
coat   so deep in mud

the woods do lie, the frost
does cover an old hut
the winds do seem to push the moon

along   or is it the clouds
first moving   or the blood
on everything that he ever loved

& prays now that it soon be ended:
finis moon & finis little world
below the moon

[pause]

FISHL'S SONG

I have no more to live for
—the dead man says—
I leave you with a curse, damned others

& may my voice be true to it
who know no kindly light
but in my death have altered

into a wolf
whose mouth is raw with blood
a ring of blood

covering my beard & throat:
a number larger than the moon
searing my chest

conflated,
still,
opens to let the spirit out

DI TOYTE KLOLES (THE MALEDICTIONS)

Let the dead man call out in you because he is a dead man

Let him look at your hands in the light that filters through the table
where he sits

Let him tell you what he thinks & let your throat gag on his voice

Let his words be the poem & the poem be what you wouldn't say
yourself

Let him say that every man is a murderer & that he is a murderer like
all the rest

Let him say that he would like to beat & kill beat & kill let him say
that it is nothing nothing nothing

That he is living in a wilderness (let him say it) but that there are no
woods or trees

That whatever houses there were are gone or if the houses are there
he cannot enter them or see them

That he cannot see the children that he knows were there that he
doesn't know if his own children were there too

That he seeks out the children of his enemy & would like to kill them

Let those who sit around you hear nothing of what he says let them
hear everything of what you tell them

Let a great pain come up into your legs (feel it moving like the earth
moving beneath you)

Let the earth drop away inside your belly falling falling until you're
left in space

Let his scream follow you across the millennia back to your table

Let a worm the size of a small coin come out of the table where you're
sitting

Let it be covered with the red mucus falling from his nose (but only
you will see it)

Let the holes in his body drop open let his excretions pour out across
the room

Let it flood the bottoms of the women's cages let it drip through the cracks into the faces of the women down below

Let him scream in a language you cannot understand let the word "khurbn" come at the end of every phrase

Let a picture begin to form with every scream

Let the screams tell you that the world was formed in darkness that it ends in darkness

Let the screams take you into a room with small white tiles

Let the tiles vanish beneath the press of bodies let vomit & shit be everywhere let semen & menstrual blood run down his arms

Let his screams describe a body (a body is like a stone a body rests on another body & weighs it down a body crushes the skull that lies beneath it a body has arms & reaches for the sky a body has eyes & knows terror in the darkness a body burning gives off heat & light)

Let 10,000 bodies be gathered in one place until they vanish let the earth & sky vanish with them & then return

Let an empty field fill up with coins & let the living bend to pick them up

Let everything have its price let there be a price for death & a price for life so that everything can be accounted

Let them account the value of a body (a soul has no account) & let the living refuse the living unless a price is paid

Let betrayal take the place of love & let disgust be put ahead of beauty

Let she who is most beautiful be brought down to her knees let those who hold together out of love be murdered

Let the dead cry for the destruction of the living until there is no more death & no more life

Let a ghost in the field put out the light of the sun (I have no arms he cries

My face & half my body have vanished & am I still alive?

But the movement of my soul through space & time brings me inside you

The immeasurable part of a language is what we speak he says who
am I? dayn mamas bruder farshvunden in dem khurbn un muz in
mayn eygenem loshn redn loz mikh es redn durkh dir dos vort
khurbn
Mayne oygen zaynen blind fun mayn khurbn ikh bin yetst a peyger)
a corpse to which the light will not return forever for whom the
light is lost
Let the light be lost & the voices cry forever in the dark & let them
know no joy in it
Let murders multiply & tortures let fields rot & forests shrink let
children dig up bones under the market square
Let fools wield power let saints & martyrs root up money in a field of
blood
Let madness be the highest virtue let rage choke all who will not rage
Let children murder children let bombs rain down let houses fall
Let ghosts & dibbiks overwhelm the living
Let the invisible overwhelm the visible until nothing more is seen or
heard

---

dayn mamas bruder farshvunden...: your mother's brother vanished in the khurbn and must
speak in my own tongue let me speak it through you the word khurbn // My eyes are blind
from my khurbn I am now a corpse.

PERORATION FOR A LOST TOWN

[May 1988]: "On this road thou camest . . ."

1

what will I tell you sweet town?
that the sickness is still in you
that the dead continue to die
there is no end to the dying?
for this the departed would have had an answer:
a wedding in a graveyard
for you sweet town
they would have spoken they who are no longer among us
& would have shown forth in their splendor
would have danced pellmell
over your stones sweet town
the living & the dead together   feathers
would have blown like feathers
from their fingers   no   like gold   like roses
like every corny proposition
fathers or uncles ever gave us   they gave us
to call your image back to life
sweet town their voices twittering
like bats over your little houses
is this the sound then that the breath makes
in its final gasp that the dead make
having lived a whole life under water
now coming up for air, to find themselves
in poland in the empty field
bathers who had their bodies torn apart
& ran from you   their long guts
hanging, searching the forgotten woods
for houses & the consolation
that death brings   children in a circle

dancing   without tongues   the meadow that had once stood
    open
shut in remembrance now sweet town
the screams of the cousins carried by the wind
lost in the gentile cities
in the old men's dreams of you
each night sweet town who rise up from their beds
like children   bellowing   their words
stuck in their beards like honey
who drift up brok street past the russian church
the doctor's house beside it heavy
& whitebricked in the dream   who glide above
napoleon square o little orchards little park
where lovers once walked with lovers   children
still capture fishes in thy little pond
its surfaces still green with algae
o sounds of church bells—bimbom—through the frozen air
that call forth death o death o pale photographer
o photos of the sweet town rubbed with blood
o of its streets the photographs its vanished folk
o wanderers who wandered o bodies of the distant dead who
    stayed
o faces o dimming images lost smiles o girls embracing girls
in deathless photographs   o life receding
into images of life   you beautiful & pure   sweet town
I summon & I summon thee to answer

2

I have come here looking for the bone of my grandfather (I said).
Daylight had intervened. The town was no more empty as we walked
its length. Then the old man spat—gently—through his beard. I have
come here looking for the bone of my son. (Had someone reported a

breath of life under his houses—a movement within the soil like worms & caterpillars?) Tell the Poles that they should come to me. I am a baker & a child. I have no one to take me from this darkness.

Then he asked—or was it I who asked or asked *for* him?—were there once Jews here? Yes, they told us, yes they were sure there were, though there was no one here who could remember. What was a Jew like? they asked. (The eye torn from its socket hung against his cheek.) Did he have hair like this? they asked. How did he talk—or did he? Was a Jew tall or short? In what ways did he celebrate the Lord's day? (A rancid smell of scorched flesh choked us.) Is it true that Jews come sometimes in the night & spoil the cows' milk? Some of us have seen them in the meadows—beyond the pond. Long gowns they wear & have no faces. Their women have sharppointed breasts with long black hairs around the nipples. At night they weep. (Heads forced in the bowls until their faces ran with excrement.) No one is certain still if they exist. (Plants frozen at the bottom of a lake, its surface covered by thick ice.)

They spoke & paused. Spoke & paused again. If there was a history they couldn't find it—or a map. The cemetery they knew was gone, the dead dispersed. (On summer days the children digging in the marketplace might come across a bone.) And the shops? we asked. The stalls? The honey people? Vanished, vanished in the earth, they said. The red names & the flower names. The pink names. (There was a people once, they said, we called the old believers. A people with black beards & eyes like shriveled raisins. Out of the earth they came & lived among us. When they walked their bodies bent like yours & scraped the ground. They had six fingers on each hand. Their old men had the touch of women when we rubbed against them. One day they dug a hole and went back into the earth. They live there to this day.)

The village pump you spoke about still stands back of the city hall (they told us). The rest was all a dream.

3
[by gematria]

a wheel
dyed red

an apparition

set apart

out of the furnace

Ostrów-Mazowiecka
Poland/1988

THE BURNING BABE

The trees bring forth sweet Ecstasy
To all who in the desart roam
Till many a City there is Built
And many a pleasant Shepherd's home

But when they find the frowning Babe
Terror strikes thro the region wide
They cry the Babe the Babe is Born
And flee away on Every side

—W.B., *"The Mental Traveller"*

FOR THE GOD OF EUROPE
Poems with Variations & Coda

1
The Vision

along the road he saw
a row of babes
brightly implanted   singing
babes in many colors
red & blue & yellow
was a fantasy of babes & lights
whose eyes spelled europe
& were bright with blood
a chorus muttering forgotten names of god
whose leader was the arch babe
chewing at his mother's breast
a tiny hand upraised in grandeur
gloved & regal
he who would place a ring upon the finger
of his willing bride
pale katerina playing with her child wheel
that she offers up to him
from window of a passing train
the picture of a babe
with glaring eyes
& fingers tightly pressed
against the scepter
held in one hand
& a ball held in the other
by a babe

2

The Marriage of Saint Catherine

the groom
a babe
in bright green shirt   *after Lorenzo Venziano*
& red cape
with a red sun overhead
& dark blue moon
when they have come together
nightly in the dark
& staring at herself inside the mirror
of his god eyes
what will she do to please him
how will the pressures of her body
rest on him
her breathing filling up the nursery
the crib in which he stands
or will a babe
hands cupped   go mad
with pleasure

3

Variation & Coda

babes with yellow eyes cry out their names the mother draws a ring
around each child a picture of a risen babe with scepter grasped between
his fingers he whose train she holds unfolding it in grandeur & the
arch babe joins the chorus under blue lights rows of babes each with
a ball to bounce with eyes that stare out of a window at the waiting
bride her hand clutched in the leader's red with the blood of babes
that stains the road the babe's hand playing with her wheel one finger
on her breast he is the god of europe spinning fantasies & colors in a
vision that won't end

& from his crib in which the pressures of the dark so weigh on him that he no longer can distinguish red from green the babe wrapped in her cape feels the moon sinking in his eyes the nursery aglow with pleasures that can change a red groom to a blue god breathing lightly on his hands his marriage shirt emblazoned with the sun that's now a mirror into which he stares & sees himself reflected as before in the body of a babe

THE BURNING BABE

1
the babe
is infant boy
he sings

he is so regular
his arms grow feathers
& he flies into your dream

& lost from sight
he sails among the dead
the dear departed

little king
how many times will we
still muddle through

& fit as any fiddle
ride with you
lamb in pursuit of lamb

into a babe's world
bright & brutal
raising a hand to strike

& watching how
your own hand
trembling

bursts
like worlds emerging
into flame

2
after Southwell

a pretty babe
in air
aglow & glittering

his skin split
from the heat, his tears
a flood

but useless
cannot quench the flames
but feeds them

newly born
& burns like babe
like lamb on spit

he cries but no one
hears or feels
the heat he feels

his breast a furnace
fuelled by redhot thorns
that make him cry out

"blameless love
"o sighs & fires
"smoke & ashes

"shame & scorn
"the flames of angry justice
"mercy's hungry smile

a babe dissolved
like molten iron
casts himself

into a pit
where others fall
& vanish

bathed with blood

BLAKE'S BABES: A PROPHECY

1
infant encoil'd
inside a worm

2
The Throne of Mary

throne of wisdom
on which
the babe sits

he holds
a little sign marked
EGO

3
Pity

a flying horse
swoops down
a rider scoops
the babe up
in his arms

4
Eve

she gnaws the apple in
the serpent's mouth

5
Behold this Midnight Glory;
Worlds, on Worlds.

(Edward Young, *Night Thoughts*)

TO THE BABE IN GLORY

1
a babe
with eyes that spin

like rockets
& a flaming tongue

how cruel he is
who clamps down on

the virgin's flesh—
absent all hope

2
the babe in artaud's dream
offers his vial
of sperm   the country
rages, sending forth babes
to stoke its flames

3
a threat more than
a god-send

tearing flesh asunder
he will rise

in fury
strike his head against

the nearest wall
& totter

to the mother
who will worship him

& what he gives
will treat with

reveries of
tender love

4
babes watch
their killers
little eyes gone white

with fingers squeezed around
a doll whose eyes
are also white

& filled with
killers' faces
like a babe's

NEDJAR'S ANGELS
Paris/2001

babe fallen
sails through space
wrecked angel

babe in womb
is goat   is feeble bird
is shadow of a babe

is skull
is broken hand
is snake

babe gagged
& blind
babe under water

sewn in bag
& cast
onto the cinders

is this man
your god?
this man-child?

no one will respond
& no one
will stay whole

a babe will cry out
coldly
from the ground:

curse god & die

NEW ALTAR PIECES 2006
A Virgin with a Child

five holes in his chest—
the center one bleeding

& the face of the mother
dumbly looks out

with a towel in hand
—like a scroll   (Giovanni da Modena)

.

The Babe

head swollen
sits
on mother's lap

he reaches for
a pomegranate   (Andrea di Giusto)

.

Magdalene
stripped naked
surrounded by a troop
of babes   (Giovanni Pedrini)

.

mother & babe
sit on a rainbow like
a feathered serpent   (Giovanni da Bologna)

or on a cherub's wing   (Andrea di Bartolo)

.

dead christ
sustained by two cherubs
one raises his skirt
to show his sex   (Gerolamo da Treviso)

.

babe's foreskin,
severed,
makes a ring he places
on the finger of
his willing bride

.

Mary Magdalene
goes up to heaven

naked & surrounded
by a gang of babes

entangled in
her flowing hair   (Marco D'Oggiono)

.

Mother & Child

above them hangs
an egg
or pearl of some great price
emerging from a seashell   (Piero della Francesca)

.

Babe
stands in the sky
where once the father stood
his foot
atop the dove
& with a cross
in hand   (Timoteo Viti)

.

[Mantua: Palazzo Ducale]

sleeping babe
with snakes
around his hips

.

Pelican
above the cross
offers its blood
to feed its babes

.

In Mantegna's Room

above our heads
the gods are gone
the babes look down
from heaven
with a single bird
& laugh at us

babes with wings
of butterflies

.

after Mantegna

babe holds an apple
penis pointed at you—
will he piss?

.

[Palazzo Te]

babes in clothes
of leaves
& fish & pelican
& iron glove
& ship in flames
& porpoises
& metal door jambs
& a lonely tower

.

In a Time of War

Death with dried dugs
carrying a babe

*A bird's head on a body
of bare bones*

Death in a time of war   (Stefano della Bella)

FROM A BOOK OF CONCEALMENTS

1

RIGHTING AN ANCIENT WRONG

The way her knee swells
& she feels it
swelling & it turns into
a babe's head.
No one has a countenance
more rich
& no one has a mouth
that opens wider,
lets a sound like
dreaming come into
the room in which
they wait. So practical
it is to ride on air
to be a man or woman
growing wings
righting an ancient wrong
or casting a new spell
to trap the dead.
A chemistry
without a cause
theirs is a metamorphosis
for two. Soon
they switch their sex
like light bulbs,
practice with their eyes
& tongues, the work
of perfect strangers.
In her mouth his finger

finds a pearl
the object of his search
& bags it.
Bulbous are her cheeks
like melons   singular
her inclinations.
Cream runs from her nipples
turns into a powder
cotton candy   papa's beard
sweet as your own.
She will not let you ever
press her down
but cries for baubles
in her pensive way.
She is ready for snow
now that it's over.

2

LARGER THAN LIFE

The image & the word
over your bed
hang crucified.
The rain fades over Europe.
Men & angels
dance before the sun,
a dead snake
dangles
from a tree,
the babe
with glaring eyes
stamps on a half-chewed

apple. Happy days!
The radio is playing
songs our mothers sang,
leaving their minds
at rest.
The boy beside her bed
waits for *her* hand
to rest in *his*,
her lips to form the words
once muted
now erupting in a sigh.
The monitors who tell the time
signal time's ending,
no one alive or dead
to witness, no one
ready to ascend the wall
to scrub the image of
the god until it
vanishes but leaves
a stain behind
a kind of harbinger
larger than life.

3
LET IT BE ICE

Let it be
ice. Let ice
be the measure
of dying.
Let time
stand still &

be done.
In the wink of an eye
it is summer. The man
with his house on his back
rushes by. It is long
past our caring.
Let air mix with
air. Let those
who are dry
try water. Those
who are blind
find the sun. They are dear
to your heart.
They draw nigh.
The sun & the moon dance
& blow trumpets.
Let the earth hide
their blood, let a place
be found for
their cry. In the night
men go fishing for stars,
not a god but a babe
wields the trident.
Cables lie covered with
smut. Light erupts
on a screen. What you see
is your face   & the face
that you see, old
& blind,
is a face from
your dreams.

4

WHAT BELIEVERS SEE

The barkers stand
on the embarcadero,
black shirts
almost white from
sunlight, almost
buried in your mind,
blind in the day
but in the night
like true believers
seeing
what believers
see   the comedy of god
cloaked as a babe
the clucking of the lucky rich
among the luckless,
clocks & death their password.
Nothing gained
is nothing ventured.
Nothing cooked is nothing raw.
Marrano nights are
christian days.
Life has no chance
where white is black,
hot cold.
How warm it gets,   *for Robert Duncan, "Passages 13"*
a hand in which a coin
burns   like a foot
in bronze, its underside
the purling covers.
A plash upsets the earth,

it loosens,
smells arise a jump away
from where it stands.
First it is old
& later it is new.
Now is the fire passage
named 13.

5

THE MYSTERY OF EVIL
for Oda Makoto

The mystery of evil
rests in God,
no less in terror.
Fathers who shun the world
cry scandal
where they spawn,
eyes dark as dungeons,
a wool beard
on every face.
Men grow transparent
in their rages,
oblivious the more
they claw with
longing
at each other's flesh.
The mystery of terror
rests in God,
no less in evil.
Poems are written
to the dead,

the ones
who do not speak nor share
a common language.
In the air of caves
a figure like a god
lies broken.
His glasses tumble to the ground.
His breath smells sweet to everybody.
Fools find places
where they track the stalkers,
legs that cross a line,
a line that dwindles to a point,
a point that shatters.
Stars collide.
The words of poems
go up in smoke.
Mothers brandish babes
like weapons.
There is no
boundary dividing
life from art.

"A BABE SITS PLACIDLY IN SCHWITTERS' BAU"

. . . .

a babe sits placidly in schwitters' bau
now burnt but saved in memory
the center of a column
that his german hands sealed up
& makes me think
of dolls & dwarfs small metal cars
from childhood buttoned shoes
that fit imperfectly a walk between
high walls of buildings painted white
& nowhere have I seen
a door or found a street to turn into
escaping from the stillness of the moment
as if death wasn't an option
but a fact my mind had never entertained
till now the babe arisen looming up
then crawling where a gang of babes waits
where they fill the air with apples
thrown against the sky *the devil in the details*
hitting the old mother topsyturvy
in her falling down *o ravissement o subterfuge*
& lost in wonder a belief that time is endless
that we follow in its tracks like children
bound never to reach the place where nuns & bishops
dance to strains of monk & satie
where the taste of warm beer
fills their mouths & ours
cigarettes aglow in lost cafes
in flow of talk so rapid that the mind
grows numb the father pulls a dove

out of his hat a stick & water glass beside it
& the sky as slick as silver fills with doves
the babe with swollen head can wave at
making some stop cold
& drop to earth the plumage at their necks
once white now red with blood
& ants inside their eyes a silent army
like all armies massed for murder
& the ball that rolls across the square
finds no one there to grasp it
but it lies there fading in the sun & rain
remembered from a photograph
shot from a hundred miles in space
& bleeding salty at the edges
where the walkers pass
out of your line of sight a blur
of children's faces shrunken
without teeth or fingers
punished for the fact of childhood
now surrendered to the babe in heaven
helter skelter bowing to his will
the little master of past lives
sad king who wears a bonnet
whom the mother wheels around
in carriage words of warning
written large along its sides declaring
JESUS KILLS the voice of someone
crying in the wilderness
the butcher's hand raised with a knife
to strike the final blow the babe
a real babe now & powerless
while from a window like a jail's
above his head a false babe

has the scene in view his whirling eyes
are cameras poorly focused red
& green & purple
partner to your love & partner
to the task of bearing witness
the discovery of an age when all
was lost when even time itself
not being counted   had no meaning
but only mindless space on which
no voyager had cast a thought
no babe had come to birth or knowledge
& no schwitters made a monument
to misery that eats into the flesh
that procreates a life of pain
& pleasure where the babe who springs forth
grows to be the man   the man becomes
the voyager   the voyager no less a man
than you becomes the bearer of sad tidings
playground rumbles anxious nights
beneath the stars the city not a playpen
but a temple   home to babes & crones
the sad fragility of towers bright against the sky
no babe can yet survive in
but they tremble belch & bottom down
the blind & lame who fill our streets
the fate of merzbaus spread over the earth
the powder from their walls a distant cloud
from hannover to oslo columns rising up
in each a babe's head reaching to the room
in which we sit we are the witnesses
ourselves from dresden to new york
from ambleside to hiroshima
guernica to auschwitz

where they grind their poems into the dirt
a passage from their time to ours
khurbn shoah holocaust
a new millennium for fools new monuments
for babes & bearded prophets worship
deadlier than unbelief the battle lines invisible
in which you are the child again the father
mad to drive the mice out of your home
the center of your paradise a looming babe
arisen reaching through the ruins
for a place to soar

2001–2006

POSTFACE

The word *diaspora* arises in my mind, triggers a series of connections to which I had been late in coming, & colors the range of these poems as I now look back at them. That is what makes a *postface*, the chance to remember for myself what no one else can think or say for me. I am among the dispersed, the dispossessed—like all of us—not from any particular homeland but feeling the scattering-abroad inside me, the meaning of *diaspora* coursing through my veins. Along with that— as it did for our friend & brother-poet Edmond Jabès—the word *Jew* came out of the depths, where it had lain hidden, some three or four decades ago. In 1967, following a curious interlude & meeting with Paul Celan in Paris (I had been the first to translate him into English), I felt a rush of words & images (spent images, I thought) that wove themselves around a distant Poland peopled by Jewish specters that I first imagined & then fleshed out from others' memories & writings. The opening poem came almost by itself but for the rest I used what- ever tactics—experimental/avant-garde & otherwise—that were then at my disposal. I was deeply aware of *holocaust* but almost never spoke of it as such, knowing that I had it anyway & that I couldn't dislodge it as a hidden subtext. Another subtext, coming to surface in my mind, was a running translation into Yiddish—not a real translation but a pretended voicing in which I dreamed of myself as "the last Yiddish poet." And for what David Meltzer later called my "surrealist Yiddish vaudeville" & what I spoke of on my own as "a world of Jewish mys- tics, thieves, & madmen," I took 1931, my birth year—in New York, not Poland—as the imagined time in which to set an equally imagined "Poland."

Over the next two decades & into the present, that world continued to shadow my work, which simultaneously drove me into other geographies & ethnicities, both real & imagined. I had in that process almost successfully evaded what was, after all, the dark side of diaspora, letting some of its blackness seep through in *A Big Jewish Book* (a.k.a. *Exiled in the Word*) & in poems & experiences among & about American Indians & those Dada fathers who foretold a new poetry & art between the ruins of the two world wars. I had as yet no outlet & no voice for holocaust, & I felt that my most radical/experimental means, as I employed them elsewhere, gave me no license here. It was only in 1987, when I made the first of two trips to Poland, that the horror of the Jewish holocaust, which had been gnawing at me from childhood, sprang up from the Polish ground, or so it seemed, & took hold of me against all inclination to resist it. As the earlier work had issued from the key words "Jews" & "Poland," what began to speak through me now was incited by the Yiddish/Hebrew word *khurbn*—the familiar/familial word remembered from childhood for what later & more universally came to be called *holocaust*. This seemed more particular to my own sense of it, & it gave me, more than I had ever known it before, the feeling that I was only a vessel through which a voice or voices other than my own were speaking. What was needed further, once the work had started, was a way to channel—in no mystical sense—other voices that would help to tell the fuller story. As with *Poland/1931*, I entered on a kind of investigative poetry—the words of the true witnesses mixed with my own—& a turn to collage to put it all in place. It was this attempt at objectification—along with the poems' common themes—that marked the segue between the two works—the first one in the late 1960s & the other in 1987 & 1988.

By now another two decades have passed, & what was then close to the surface has found a deeper place in my mind. Moving into the new century, I haven't lost sight of diaspora & holocaust but come to feel them now as exile & suffering on an almost universal scale. In no sense religious I had drawn freely in *Poland/1931* on the figure of

God's exiled female aspect—Shekinah—while in *Khurbn* the over-whelming imagery for me was that of emptiness & silence. With *Poland*, looking back, I could indulge a high degree of play in a way I couldn't or wouldn't in the case of *Khurbn*. The years after *Khurbn* brought that back to me, but the central image this time was the Babe—the infant, like Christ, as god & victim. I began to feel this too—to feel the poems in which it issued—as the climax to what had come to me with *Poland* & again with *Khurbn*—the absurdity & horror of the god-child as that figure entered my imaginings. The weirdness came first & drew me to a history of images whose power & sometime sensuality were still present at both the margins & center of the Christian world. These I found in wanderings through churches & museums & monasteries—babes in marvelous configurations: crowned & armored, swollen, bleeding, blind, bejewelled, feathered & recumbent, wedded often to a saint, in one uncanny instance to a serpent. But stranger (stronger) still—for me, for others—was the deformation of the Babe when set into a Jewish focus or pictured through the fearsome words of certain Christian poets—Blake in "The Mental Traveller," Southwell in "The Burning Babe", others like Levertov & Duncan from then to now. That much was literature, but the other, more awful reality was in the world outside the poem. Here, as with *Khurbn*, my impulse to play came up against what denials & murders play—the burnt & mutilated babe(s) not only as the Jewish horror but in the wreck of the divine when brought low anywhere by murder & by "holocaust" (itself a death by burning) that has haunted us down to the very present. For the depiction of these the Babe is a spent image & a companion as such to the spent images that life & the life of poetry must constantly absorb. The terminal point for me was the 2001 devastation in New York, to which I was a nearby witness, but fused here with a memory of Kurt Schwitters' sculptural *Merzbau*, destroyed (also by fire) in World War Two. The column at its center, on top of which a babe's head was implanted, serves me for a reprise & a coda.

INDEX OF TITLES

ACKNOWLEDGMENTS

Poland/1931 originally appeared in a separate edition published by New Directions in 1974, and *Khurbn* was part of the volume *Khurbn & Other Poems*, 1989, also published by New Directions. Some of the poems from *The Burning Babe* were issued in a limited edition of that title with illuminations by Susan Bee, published by Granary Books, New York, in 2005. Grateful acknowledgment is also made to the editors and publishers of the following magazines and anthologies in which some of the materials in this volume were previously published:

POLAND/1931: *Action Poétique: l'anthologie* (Paris), *America a Prophecy* (ed. J. Rothenberg and G. Quasha), *American Literary Anthology 3*, *Anonym*, *Caterpillar*, *A Caterpillar Anthology* (ed. C. Eshleman), *Choice*, *Corpus*, *Coyote's Journal*, *Damascus Road*, *European Judaism* (London), *From the Other Side of the Century* (ed. D. Messerli), *Ikon*, *Imago* (Montreal), *Intrepid*, *Io*, *Laugh Literary and Man the Humping Guns*, *The Nation*, *The New American Poetry* (ed. D. Allen and G. Butterick), *New Directions in Prose and Poetry 28*, *Open Poetry* (ed. G. Quasha and R. Gross), *Poetry Review* (London), *Postmodern American Poetry: A Norton Anthology* (ed. P. Hoover), *Preferences* (ed. Thomas Victor), *Response*, *Salon* (Olomouc, Czech Republic), *Sixpack*, *some/thing*, *Stars & Stripes: americka poezija postmodernizma antologija* (Split, Croatia), *Stony Brook*, *Sumac*, *Sumac Anthology*, *Telling and Remembering: A Century of American Jewish Poetry* (ed. Steven J. Rubin), *Tractor*, *Transpacific*, *Tree*, *Unmuzzled Ox*, *Vice Versa* (Mexico).

KHURBN: *American Poets on the Holocaust* (ed. Charles Fishman), *Después de Auschwitz* (J. Rothenberg translated by Mercedes Roffé), *Ergo*, *Geschichte Leben* (Berlin), *Jewish American Literature: A Norton*

Anthology, Jewish American Poetry: Poems, Commentary, and Reflections (ed. J. N. Barron and E. M. Selinger), *New Directions in Prose and Poetry 52, Novi Pesnicki Poredak:Antologia novije americke poezije* (Novi Sad, Serbia), *Nuova poesia americana* (Milan, ed. P. Vangelisti and L. Ballerini), *Poems for the Millennium* (ed. J. Rothenberg and P. Joris), *Shirim, Sulfur, Telling and Remembering: A Century of American Jewish Poetry* (ed. Steven J. Rubin), *Temblor, Tempestad* (Mexico), *Trópico* (Sao Paolo), *Verbigracia* (Caracas).

THE BURNING BABE: *Alligatorzine* (Belgium), *Bombay Gin, 5-Trope, Golden Handcuffs Review, Helicon* (Israel), *Poets Against the War* (online), *Princeton University Library Chronicle, Skanky Possum, Un livre des recels* (J. Rothenberg, translated by Yves Di Manno).

Illustration credits for *Poland/1931*: collage page 2 (1967) by Eleanor Antin; photograph, page 30, by Laurence Fink; postal cards, pages 50 and 100, and collage, page 82, courtesy of the author; artwork, page 118, by the author; artwork, page 138 by Michael Manfredo.

If any other acknowledgments have been omitted, it is unintentional and forgiveness is requested.